# The Essentia.

## Understanding the stock market through the price-earnings ratio

by Keith Anderson

**Hh**

HARRIMAN HOUSE LTD

3A Penns Road
Petersfield
Hampshire
GU32 2EW
GREAT BRITAIN

Tel: +44 (0)1730 233870
Fax: +44 (0)1730 233880
Email: enquiries@harriman-house.com
Website: www.harriman-house.com

First published in Great Britain in 2012

978-0-85719-080-2

British Library Cataloguing in Publication Data
A CIP catalogue record for this book can be obtained from the British Library.

Printed and bound in Great Britain by Marston Book Services Limited, Oxfordshire

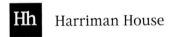 Harriman House

# Contents

Acknowledgements                                                    v

About the Author                                                   vii

Foreword: Werner De Bondt                                           ix

Preface                                                           xiii

Introduction                                                        xv


**PART I: The P/E Calculation**                                      **1**

Chapter 1. History of the P/E                                        5

Chapter 2. Earnings                                                 11

Chapter 3. The Price-Earnings Ratio (P/E)                           19

Chapter 4. Practical Calculation of EPS and the P/E from
            Company Accounts                                        27


**PART II: The Value Premium and the P/E**                          **33**

Chapter 5. Value Investing                                          37

Chapter 6. Efficient Markets and the CAPM                           51

Chapter 7. Accepting Reality: The Fama and French 3-Factor Model    63

Chapter 8. Value Investors Fight Back                               69


**PART III: Improving the P/E**                                     **75**

Chapter 9. Developing the P/E                                       79

Chapter 10. The PEG Ratio                                           85

Chapter 11. The Long-Term P/E                                       95

Chapter 12. Decomposing the P/E                                    105

Chapter 13. A Cautionary Tale: The Naked P/E                       119

Chapter 14. Have We Rescued the P/E?                               129

## PART IV: Beyond the P/E                                     133

Chapter 15. Ben Graham: The P/E and the Margin of Safety        137

Chapter 16. Joel Greenblatt: The P/E and Return on Capital      143

Chapter 17. Joseph Piotroski: The P/E and the Fscore            149


## Conclusion                                                  165

## Appendices                                                  171

FTSE 100 EPSs and P/Es                                          173

Glossary                                                        177

References                                                      187

## Index                                                       191

# Acknowledgements

I would like to thank Richard Beddard for the huge contribution he made to earlier drafts of this book, and Stephen Eckett and Suzanne Anderson at Harriman House for the original suggestion, their support and patience. Thanks also to Werner DeBondt for agreeing to write the foreword. Along with Ben Graham's *The Intelligent Investor* and David Dreman's books, his 1985 paper with Richard Thaler *Does the Stock Market Overreact?* convinced me early on that misvaluation can be rife, even in a mostly efficient market.

# About the Author

After completing his BSc in Mathematical Statistics and Operational Research at Exeter, Keith Anderson worked for some years as a systems developer, most recently at Deutsche Bank in Frankfurt. He then did an MSc in Investment Analysis at Stirling, where he won the Morley Prize as the top academically in his year. For his PhD at the ICMA Centre, Reading University, Keith showed that different ways of calculating the price–earnings ratio could significantly improve investor returns.

He worked as a lecturer at Durham University Business School for two years before moving to York in 2008.

# Foreword: Werner De Bondt

Hardly any topic in finance has been explored as much as the relationship between value and price. One way is to examine the ratio of the share price of a company to its annual earnings per share, called the *P/E ratio*. Data from several markets indicate that stocks with low P/E ratios (so-called value firms) earn significantly higher returns than high P/E stocks (i.e., growth or glamour companies). This book joins the discussion about why this happens.

Many observers would agree that every so often investors go mad and that asset prices overshoot. Stock prices are regularly either too high or too low relative to what can be justified by business fundamentals (say, the company's earning power). The breakdown occurs both at the market level and at the level of individual securities. The experience of the last few years leaves no doubt that speculative bubbles in equity, debt, real estate, and other markets may cause immense harm to the world economy. Irrational exuberance has proven to be extremely disruptive. Nonetheless, routine everyday mis-pricing in the cross-section of securities also offers interesting profit opportunities for stock market investors.

In this volume, Dr. Keith Anderson presents an expert summary of past research on P/E ratios and investment strategy. He also contributes to the existing literature in behavioral asset pricing with an array of statistical analyses that employ U.K. data. What's more, Anderson's book has practical use. He explains how traders can execute a winning P/E strategy.

In my view, there is no reason to worry that the success of P/E investing will diminish over time. Still, traditional P/E ratios do have limits. Anderson makes clear how one can adjust P/E ratios and turn them into even more powerful predictors of future returns, while controlling for risk. I am certain that many readers will benefit from this insightful book. I admire what the author has accomplished.

Anderson's empirical analysis and practical advice extend a line of scientific investigation stretching back 80 years. For decades, it was thought that movements in stock prices are random. Paradoxically, most researchers interpreted the unpredictability of returns as proof of the rationality of Wall Street. In an efficient market, prices must reflect all information quickly and accurately. If the hypothesis is true, only news that takes people by surprise – and that is as likely to be positive as negative – can have an impact on prices.

Even so, most amateur and professional investors continued to study financial reports and relied on trading rules in hopes of attaining superior portfolio performance. *Security Analysis*, the investors' bible co-authored by Benjamin Graham and David Dodd in 1934, spelled out some of the specific methods that could be used, including P/E ratios. *Security Analysis* sold nearly a million copies. Later, in 1949, Graham also published *The Intelligent Investor*, a more concise book that is still in print today and that reviews basic investment principles in a form suitable for laymen. It was *The Intelligent Investor* that introduced the P/E ratio to the public at large.

For a long time, Graham and his followers were unable to convince the academic world to abandon its efficient markets dogma and rational worldview.[1] Since the late 1970s, however, new statistical studies, meticulously executed, have found that there are definite patterns in stock prices and that price and value may drift apart. So, the efforts of investors do not have to be futile, as predicted by the theory of efficient markets. For instance, there are trends in equity returns after earnings announcements. Surely, the most prominent behavioral anomaly relative to the classical theory of finance is the P/E effect discussed here.

The predictability in returns is connected to the remarkable volatility of market prices, itself linked to rapid surges and sudden stops in trading volume. Major fluctuations in stock prices usually go together with broadly anticipated changes in corporate earnings that may or may not be realized a few years later. Thus, P/Es are indicators of expected future earnings growth. Alas, too many people wrongly

---

[1] There are some noteworthy exceptions. John Burr Williams argued in *The Theory of Investment Value* that security prices are based "too much on current earning power, too little on long-run dividend paying power" (1938, p. 19). Also with the boom of the 1920s and the later crash in mind, John Maynard Keynes noted in *The General Theory* that "day-to-day fluctuations in the profits of existing investments, which are obviously of an ephemeral and non-significant character, tend to have an altogether excessive, and even an absurd, influence on the market" (1936, pp. 153-154). Even earlier, William Stanley Jevons said that "as a general rule, it is foolish to do just what other people are doing, because there are almost sure to be too many people doing the same thing."

assume short-term events to be of great consequence for the long-term outlook of individual firms and the economy as a whole. (Hence, the earnings forecasts of financial analysts tend to be too extreme.) This extrapolative bias is perhaps the main cause of market overreaction. Regardless of their objective lack of information about what will happen tomorrow, traders have strong views just the same. In addition, investor sentiment and risk perception are closely tied to recent price movements. Thus, many traders fall into the trap of buying at market high-points (an observation that suggests overconfidence and recklessness) and selling at market low-points (an observation that suggests panic).

When do exaggerated price movements reach their inevitable turning points? We do not know. Precise, well-timed forecasts are simply unattainable. Indeed, the upward or downward price momentum that is typically associated with growth and value stocks may well continue for some time. However, we do know that, once false beliefs about earnings, risk or the attitudes of other traders take hold, it usually takes a great deal of opposing news, unfolding over many months (say, a brutal string of earnings surprises), to defeat crowd sentiment. Still, in the end, more often than not, prices do turn around, and diversified portfolios of low P/E stocks earn higher returns and expose investors to less risk than portfolios of high P/E stocks.

It is a great challenge to try to improve one's investment performance, and it is especially stressful to go against majority opinion, to be a contrarian investor – even if it pays to be contrary! This book offers essential scientific reassurance, as well as practical tools, to triumph over misconceptions and behavioral errors that distort stock market prices. I recommend it to readers with great enthusiasm.

**Werner De Bondt**
Professor and Director
Richard H. Driehaus Center for Behavioral Finance
DePaul University
Chicago, Illinois
U.S.A.

# Preface

## Who is this book for?

The book is primarily aimed at investors who already know something about investing in shares, but is also suitable for market professionals and academics. Quite simply, readers should already know what a price–earnings ratio (P/E) is.

If you are a private investor, rest assured that the book assumes no prior knowledge of any particular accounting or finance terms. Everything covered is defined at the time. For more detail, many terms, in particular accounting terms, are explained in the Glossary at the back. There are however many new ideas presented, and beyond Part I even seasoned stock market investors will need to think hard.

The book is also suitable for investment analysts, fund managers or finance academics. If you have a finance MSc or MBA then you may find some of the explanations over-simplified, but you will also learn much that is new. Using the P/E to get the best investment results is far from a simple task once you get into the details, and you should also find much of interest here.

## What does the book cover?

The book starts with the basics: the fundamentals of share prices and how earnings and P/Es are calculated in the UK. I then look at the value premium, which is the whole basis of using the P/E as an investment tool: low P/E shares, on average, outperform the market. I cover some of the models that believers in efficient markets have come up with to try to explain this inconvenient fact, and why those who believe in pervasive mispricing remain unconvinced. This group of value investors includes such illustrious figures as Warren Buffett – as well as your author.

The second half of the book gets into the details of the P/E: developments that have tried to improve it, and how some famous value investors have combined it with other measures. The P/E can be made into a powerful tool. But as with most powerful tools it can run amok if you don't control it properly, check what it is telling you by looking at other statistics, and apply a liberal amount of common sense.

## Structure of the book

**Part I** introduces the surprisingly short history of the P/E. Then, for the benefit of the majority of readers who have not done an MSc in Investment Analysis, I go through in detail how earnings and then P/Es are calculated. I use motor manual publisher Haynes as the practical example throughout the book. They are small enough to have reasonably straightforward accounts yet most readers should have heard of them.

**Part II** covers the value premium and some famous investors who use it. I also look at efficient market theorists' models of how returns on stocks can be explained, some of the objections to them, and the half-way house of the popular Fama and French three-factor model.

**Part III** looks at some existing developments of the P/E such as the PEG ratio. I then go on to some of my PhD thesis work, since published as peer-reviewed academic papers and expanded and updated for this book. The P/E can be made into a much more powerful weapon in any investor's armoury by applying a few relatively simple adjustments. However, the flawed results from the Naked P/E show the importance of taking into account other statistics beyond the P/E.

This is demonstrated in **Part IV**, where I cover two famous value investors and how they have put the P/E to work with other statistics, so as to identify value shares of reliable companies. The last chapter is some more original work, showing how you can combine the P/E with an as yet little known measure of a company's financial stability to get outstanding and reliable investment results.

# Introduction

## Who needs a book on the P/E?

In recent decades the P/E has been the most important and best-known investment ratio. Indeed, apart from the share price, it is the *only* investment statistic that is published in print every day. Every share quoted in London has its P/E printed daily in the Companies section of the *Financial Times*. The P/E also has a strong intuitive meaning: it tells you how many years' worth of future earnings you are paying in order to buy the share now.

One might ask why there *hasn't* been a book before on the P/E.

On the other hand, if you are a fund manager, the P/E or something based on it will be just one of the battery of ratios you use. You will have a filter of many different investment ratios that all of your investment universe must pass. The computer does the filtering for you, and presents you with a list of all the stocks that are interesting enough to be worth investigating further. The P/E is an integral but probably minor part of that process, and you would no more expect a book on the P/E than on ROCE or EBITDA.

While the value to investors of being familiar with this widely used statistic is clear, professionals in financial markets may find it a more surprising subject, possibly never having stopped to think how or why it is calculated that way. Such professionals may well be surprised by how easily the P/E could be improved if things were done slightly differently.

## What's interesting about the P/E?

The P/E tells you how many years of future earnings you are willing to pay to own a company's shares now.

*What more is there to tell?*

I first became interested in investing my own money in the stock market over ten years ago. Bored by a comfortable but limited existence at Deutsche Bank, I took a year out to do an MSc in Investment Analysis. While I was looking round for a dissertation topic I read Graham and Dodd's 1934 classic *Security Analysis*. One of their suggestions was that you should not judge a company's earnings potential over just the last year, but take a longer term view of 7-10 years to allow for fluctuations in the economy as a whole. This seemed such a common-sense suggestion, and yet after searching through dozens of academic papers, as far as I could tell no-one had thought to test Graham and Dodd's assertion in the 70 years since. Being a new idea to the academic world the idea took a bit of explaining to my supervisor, but the results from the limited tests I was then able to do were promising.

Since then I have gone on to do a PhD in how to improve the P/E ratio as a predictor of investor returns, some of which is updated and summarised here.

The long-term P/E and decomposing the P/E are, I feel, surprisingly rich and complex stories. I have also taught much of this book's contents to some thousands of undergraduate and Masters students at Durham University and the University of York, a few of whom I hope have shared my enthusiasm.

But the story of the P/E is not a dry academic investigation. It is a practical guide to how any stock market investor can put an improved P/E to use.

## The faults of the P/E

Even a novice private investor should know that the P/E has some glaring faults. A low P/E may mean a company that has been marked down for no readily apparent reason, and thus an attractive value investment for those with the patience to wait while the market re-values it. However, the P/E is a backward-looking measure, based on one large number (sales last year) minus another large number (total costs last year). Just because the company earned £1 per share last year doesn't necessarily mean it will earn anything like that for the foreseeable future. A low P/E can also easily mean a company that is deservedly cheap because it is in financial difficulty, and that it is likely to become cheaper yet or even go into administration.

From a different point of view, in the world of academic finance the P/E has been largely forgotten as an investment ratio for researchers since the early 1990s. Its power to identify cheap shares that will perform was first shown in 1960, but in the last 15 years few papers have been written on it. The P/E has simply shown itself not to be as powerful an indicator of a value share as several other similar measures available. In particular the P/E was left out of Fama and French's three-factor model of stock returns (which I cover in Part II). This model has, in the academic world at least, become the most popular way of explaining the returns that can be expected from holding the shares of various types of company.

## Putting right the faults in the P/E

It is these failings that I seek to put right in Parts III and IV. Comparing a company's share price to its earnings is still a major basis of analysis for many value investors, but the pitfalls are numerous. This book explains how the P/E's weaknesses can be overcome.

The short-term bias of the traditional P/E is easily overcome. The fact that the P/E is largely conditioned by the overall market P/E, the company's size and the sector in which it operates, takes some rather more complicated adjustment but can still be done using freely available information. These adjustments put in your hands a tool that is much more finely tuned to revealing shares that are good value.

The other important thing the P/E does not tell you is whether a company is in trouble. As the history of the Naked P/E (explained later in the book) attests, building your portfolio on the basis of one statistic, however clever it may be, can lead to catastrophe during a market crash. Luckily, most of this risk can be avoided if you are prepared to step outside the P/E and use complementary statistics that steer you clear of the riskiest stocks. Combining the improved P/E with a measure of a company's current financial strength provides a simple yet powerful filter. The final result is a set of stocks that are both underpriced in terms of their earnings power, and also solvent and likely to remain so.

# PART I
## The P/E Calculation

This Part starts with the story of how investors came to use the P/E. It has been in use for less than a century, but during that time it has become the most important investment ratio as far as practical investors are concerned.

Chapter 2 looks at the more complicated component of the P/E: earnings. How the market decides share prices minute-by-minute is extremely complicated, but viewed from the level of the P/E calculation, the price used is quite straightforward. Earnings, however, are much more complex. There are many possible definitions of which parts of the profit and loss account are really 'last year's earnings', and I cover them in detail here.

Having defined earnings, the share price and then the price–earnings ratio itself are covered in the following chapter. As with earnings, there are several different ways of calculating the P/E.

All the theory is brought to life in this Part's final chapter, with a detailed example of how the P/E works in practice using Haynes Publishing's annual report.

# Chapter 1
## History of the P/E

*The P/E ratio is today the most commonly used valuation metric in the world.*

**Prof. Janette Rutterford, Open University, 2004**

The P/E has a long history, but it has not always been the most popular way to value shares. Since the invention of stock markets up until less than 100 years ago, the dividend yield (DY) was the main figure every investor was interested in. The asset backing behind a company was also important. The P/E is, compared to these two, a relatively recent invention. Even the phrase 'price–earnings ratio' only became popular in the 1920s in the US. In the UK dividends were still what mattered up until the mid-1960s.

## The world of investment to 1914: dividend yield is king

For centuries, at least since the time of the South Sea Bubble in 1720, dividend yield (DY) was the main ratio investors used to value their stocks. This is simply the ratio of the dividends paid out last year to the price of the stock. So if a stock costing £1 paid out 5p in dividends last year, the dividend yield of 5% compares favourably to the return available from a deposit account (in 2011), but of course involving the risk of capital loss should the share price fall.

In the US, bond issues during the 1800s and early 1900s outweighed stock issues three to one. The stock market consisted largely of railway stocks, with utilities and then industrials only becoming more important by 1900. In these circumstances it is hardly surprising that dividend yield was the favoured method of deciding whether a stock was cheap or expensive, because dividend yield could be directly compared to the yield on a bond.

In the UK, the stock market was more developed, even though the railway boom was equally active. One feature was how internationalised the stock market was: the majority of new issues was of foreign stocks and bonds. Another feature strange to a modern investor was the preponderance of debenture and preferred stocks. In a new issue from an established investment-grade company, these were often the only type of stock an investor could buy. The founders would keep control of the ordinary stock. It was speculative companies that issued ordinary shares.

Even in the UK though, DY was the main statistic that investors were interested in. This could have been due to the limited information published in what we now call an IPO (Initial Public Offering) (this term is itself only about twenty years old). The only information a purchaser of a new issue would likely get would be profits averaged over several years (to even out the ups and downs), money available to pay the ordinary dividend after paying the preferred shareholders, and the balance sheet. Given the limited information made public in those days, it is not surprising that a more sophisticated analysis of company earnings was not yet possible.

## The US in the 1920s: enter the P/E

DY in the US maintained its hold until the mid-1920s. The P/E only really became popular during the boom years of the late 1920s. Earnings themselves had boomed since the Great War. People were more interested in earnings growing at 10% or 25% annually than dividends growing at 5%. Everyone believed that this long-term growth could be kept up indefinitely due to rapid technological change. US company accounts were also generally more informative than in the UK, so that investors in US companies could see what was happening to retained earnings. They could appreciate the fact that the effect of compound interest on a company's growing reserves would mean higher dividends and hence higher share prices in the future. Ben Graham and David Dodd could already comment in their 1934 classic *Security Analysis*:

> Common stocks have come to depend exclusively on the earnings exhibit.

## Catching up with the US

Meanwhile, DY remained for decades the main valuation ratio in the UK. Earnings were overwhelmingly paid out as dividends, whereas in the US a significant proportion was held back as undistributed profits. UK corporate earnings had themselves not shown the long-term rapid growth that US companies had experienced, so the gap between the two valuation methods was not as marked.

Relatively uninformative UK company accounts did not help: consolidated accounts (reporting the group's overall position rather than individual companies within the group) were not compulsory until 1948, and even something as basic as turnover did not legally have to be disclosed until 1976. As a result you could find analysts in the same research note covering US stocks in an industry by looking mainly at their P/E, but the UK stocks in the same industry by mainly considering their DY.

It was not until 1965 that UK investors really caught up with the US in their use of valuation ratios. The introduction of corporation tax in that year meant that companies and individual shareholders were finally treated as separate taxable entities. Until then, companies had paid income tax on behalf of their investors, who might have to pay further tax depending on their level of income. Thus it was difficult to estimate company income after company taxes but before personal taxes. By 1966 *The Economist* was already valuing many UK companies using their P/Es.

## The P/E today

Amongst practical investors the P/E has maintained its popularity since then. However, there are two areas in which the P/E has been eclipsed in recent years. Interest in it from finance academics has been limited since Eugene Fama and Ken French decided in the early 1990s that price-to-book value was a better indicator of value stocks and dropped the P/E from their now widely popular three factor model. (See Chapter 7.)

The other time the P/E has become little used has been during stock market bubbles. This is ironic considering that the P/E itself only came to prominence during the 1920s' boom in the US. Some extraordinary P/E ratios occurred during the dot.com mania: America Online reached a P/E of 275 and Yahoo a P/E of 1900.

Extraordinary P/Es in the hundreds or thousands are telling investors that they are building castles in the sky, but during bubbles that is precisely the message that investors don't want to hear.

# Chapter 2
## Earnings

Before we can cover the P/E itself, we should first define its more complicated component: earnings. This chapter covers the basics of the different ways in which earnings and then earnings per share (EPS) can be defined. I move downwards through the profit and loss account and discuss the different figures as more and more costs are deducted from profits. The discussion is purposely kept general here; for a practical example, see the later chapter on Haynes. I do not intend to give a detailed explanation of company accounts, as many other books do this; I cover only the components of the earnings calculation.

## From sales to operating profit

The basics need little explanation.

A company produces goods or services and sells them; the amount the company receives here is termed the *sales* (or *turnover*, or *revenue*). From this figure of sales we need first of all to deduct the cost of the items sold to calculate the *gross profit*.

However, we have not yet reached the first figure that counts as earnings, because many expenses must be taken into account on top of raw materials, such as staff costs, IT, rent and so on. Other notional expenses, such as depreciation and amortisation, are also deducted. These are not necessarily items that have caused us to actually spend any cash this year, but they need to be deducted regularly from gross profit in any case. Declared profits would be excessively variable if large occasional expenditures on capital items were recorded as they happened. There is anyway a separate Consolidated Cash Flow statement.

'Earnings' as a word on its own is in fact a rather ill-defined catch-all term for any of the profit figures we now cover. The initial figure for earnings is the difference between revenue and the total of these costs – basically all the costs of the company excluding finance charges and tax. This initial earnings figure is called **operating profit**.

# Towards the P/E's earnings figure

Operating profit is the highest figure up the profit and loss account that is referred to as 'earnings'. However, there are two unavoidable costs of running a business that still remain to be taken out: interest paid to service loans, and tax. Subtracting interest paid gives **profit before tax**. Finally subtracting tax paid gives **profit from continuing operations**. (Details of any discontinued operations will appear in a separate column in the profit and loss account.)

Now all the necessary deductions have been made to the profit, a 'clean' figure is available to distribute to shareholders or into the company reserves. It is this profit from continuing operations that is used in EPS calculations.

# EBIT and EBITDA

These ungainly acronyms have become increasingly popular in recent years. **EBIT** stands for earnings before interest and tax, and **EBITDA** for earnings before interest, tax, depreciation and amortisation. There are times when they may legitimately be used. For example, EBITDA is often used in loan covenants, partly because the bondholders are not concerned about tax payments – interest payments are made before a company's tax liability is calculated.

However, it is hard to avoid the impression that EBIT and EBITDA have become so widely quoted because they make every company's earnings look better. It is always a bad sign to come across a company proudly quoting its EBITDA in the first few pages of graphics in its annual report, instead of profit figures from further down the profit and loss account. Often a few seconds with a calculator will show that the company has little or no chance of ever making a real profit, because its amortisation charges more than wipe out the operating profit each year.

EBIT and EBITDA have been memorably if unkindly described as "look how much we could have earned if we didn't have to pay our bills". Interest on loans and tax are unavoidable costs of running a business and really should be taken account of. If the company sourced its capital from shareholders, instead of borrowing the money, then it would presumably have to pay dividends instead of loan interest. Tax is sadly unavoidable for us all, and does at least help provide a safe legal framework in which the company can operate. Depreciation and amortisation are even more basic expenses that have already been subtracted before the operating income is reported. As Warren Buffett asked: "Does management think the tooth fairy pays for capital expenditures?" I do not use EBIT or EBITDA further here.

# Basic, diluted and adjusted EPS

Having calculated earnings with all necessary costs taken out, we can now move from the company level to the per-share level. EPS is calculated by dividing profit from continuing operations by the number of shares in issue. This is **basic EPS**.

However, the company may well have options grants outstanding to executives, and sometimes to employees too, which will vest if certain targets are attained. These give a higher number of possible shares in the future. Dividing profit by the number of all the shares that exist now or might possibly vest gives **diluted EPS**.

The figure often quoted in the financial press is **adjusted EPS** (also known as *headline EPS*). This uses earnings with exceptional items excluded – large, one-off costs such as the expense of closing down an unprofitable division. Unfortunately, the exact definition of what is classified as 'exceptional' varies by company – the company's accountants have wide latitude over the accounting figures.

# Historical, rolling and forecast EPS

Another possible dimension to the stated EPS figure is whether it is historical or forecast. **Historical EPS** is the simplest and is what has been covered above, i.e. the earnings stated in the company's most recent annual report.

**Rolling EPS** is based on the latest available earnings information. In the UK, if the six-monthly interim report has come out, the earnings from the first half of the annual report drop out and are replaced by these most recent earnings. US companies, and many large companies that are quoted in the US such as BP, declare results quarterly, so for them the rolling figure is the most recent four quarters. These six-monthly or quarterly announcements are unaudited, so unlike the figures in the annual report they are subject to review.

**Forecast EPS** does not come from the company, although they may provide guidance. It is the average of the earnings expected to be declared for the current accounting period, as forecast by the analysts who cover the company. For a large company in the FTSE 100 this will mean a dozen or more analysts' forecasts being available at any one time.

Since we are interested in the returns to be had from the company in the future, not the recent past, why do we not always use forecast EPS and forget about historic EPS? The major problem here is that forecast EPS will usually be quoted only if three or more analysts follow the company. Forecast earnings are thus available only for the few hundred largest UK companies – effectively, members of the FTSE-350 Index plus a few others. Of the roughly 1,300 trading companies quoted in London, there are hundreds with a market capitalisation of less than £50m. These are unlikely to have even three analysts covering them, particularly if they are quoted on AIM. Such companies have no forecast earnings and thus no prospective P/E figure.

Because of this limited coverage offered by forecast earnings, academic research to back-test particular trading rules invariably uses historical EPS, not forecast EPS. (The fact that you have to pay for a higher DataStream subscription level to get the analysts' forecasts, and few universities can afford to do so, may also be relevant!)

## Problems with earnings figures

There is a significant problem near the top of the profit and loss account. Operating income, being one large number (sales) minus another large number (costs), may be highly variable. Depending on the industry and business model, perfectly healthy companies may nevertheless have wafer-thin profit margins.

For example, Inchcape import and distribute thousands of cars every year. Given the huge volume of metal moving through their distribution channels, a 1% or 2% profit margin is very healthy. However a small percentage change in either sales or costs leads to a very large change in the operating income. Forecasting earnings figures for such companies is therefore a particularly error-prone business. Forecast earnings depend acutely on the assumptions made about how gross sales and total costs will change in the future.

Another sticking point when calculating earnings is that sales in any one year, and hence earnings, are easily manipulated. It was mentioned above that what is classified as an exceptional cost, and thus to be excluded from adjusted EPS, is a matter of opinion. The company's managers are likely to take a more liberal view of what costs are exceptional than a potential investor. Some large companies seem to need to close down an unprofitable division or operations in some particular country every year, but they still book it as exceptional. When this seems to happen year after year, one is entitled to ask how exceptional it really is.

A whole branch of academic finance literature exists on the manipulation of earnings and how it may be identified. The dividing line between current managers wanting to present their actions in as positive a light as possible, and fraud, is not necessarily easy to draw. Any investor who follows the market for any length of time will have read about scandals of companies booking sales before they are absolutely definite, so as to enhance the apparent performance of the sales managers responsible and thus their bonuses. A recent well-publicised case is Findel, who run Kleeneze among other businesses. In 2010 their educational supplies division was found to have been making "unsubstantiated accounting entries". Earnings had to be restated, the shares of the Group fell precipitately and have not yet recovered.

One final problem is the practical indeterminacy of EPS figures. Trying to pin down the precise basis of any particular basic, diluted, adjusted, forecast, rolling or historical EPS figure offered you is a real can of worms. Three different financial data sources, such as DataStream, the *Financial Times* and Hemmington Scott's Company REFS will likely provide three different figures for EPS. However closely you read the online help files, unless you work as one of their data analysts and are able to read the computer code you will probably never know what exactly they include and exclude in their EPS figure. Even when I have sat down with a copy of an annual report and tried to work out exactly where an EPS figure came from, I have usually been unsuccessful. However, as long as you are using the same definition for all the companies you are considering investing in, it is unlikely to be a decisive factor.

# Chapter 3
## The Price-Earnings Ratio (P/E)

Having covered earnings in considerable detail, we are finally able to use the earnings figure arrived at as one of the two inputs into the P/E calculation.

The other input is of course the share price. At the level of detail required for the P/E, the price is quickly dealt with. The figure used in the quoted P/E statistics is invariably the previous day's closing price, so unlike the EPS figure it will not vary from source to source. However, as with EPS figures there is still a certain amount of indeterminacy involved: bid, mid, offer and closing prices may all be slightly different and the method of calculation varies depending on the trading platform. The closing price may not necessarily be the price at which any shares actually changed hands. If you try to buy some shares today, the price asked by the market, and hence the P/E available, will have moved on again.

## Understanding the P/E ratio

As mentioned in Chapter 1, early in the twentieth century US investors started comparing share prices to profits: dividing the company's market capitalisation by last year's declared profits. Equivalently, at the per-share level they could divide the share price by the EPS. This gave them a rough-and-ready estimate of how many future years' earnings they were paying in order to own part of the company.

Typical P/Es encountered when the market is neither particularly high or low are in the range of 8-12, i.e. you are paying 8-12 years' worth of future earnings in order to own one share now. As we shall see in a later chapter, however, this varies according to several factors.

The average P/E of the market itself waxes and wanes with overall market confidence, as Figure 1 shows. The FTSE 100's P/E peaked at 30.5 in the technology stock boom in early 2000, but fell to a low of 7.2 at the nadir of the banking crisis in early 2009.

**Figure 1: FTSE 100 P/Es, 1993-2012**

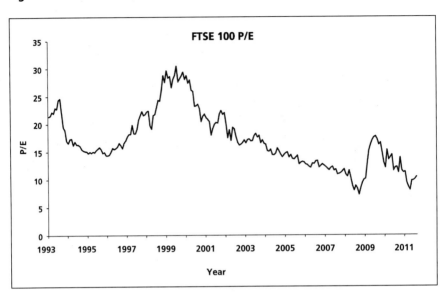

Large companies generally have higher P/Es than small companies. I am not aware of any accepted explanation for why this is. In my opinion it is probably due to the fact that fund managers investing billions have little choice but to invest in the largest companies: researching hundreds of sub-£50m companies simply isn't worth their time.

Figure 2 is a scatter plot of the market capitalisations of individual companies versus their P/Es. This is for all 974 quoted UK companies that had a P/E on one day in 2012. Due to some extreme values I have taken logarithms of all the data points.

**Figure 2: Market capitalisations versus P/Es for all UK companies (7 February 2012)**

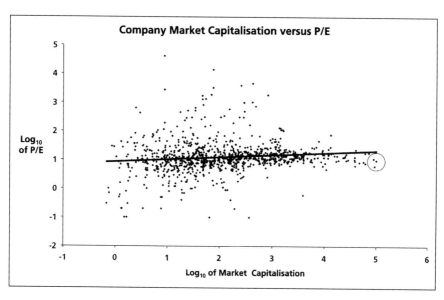

As can be seen, the P/Es do cluster around the 10-20 mark. Given that the scatter plot shows almost 1000 companies, very few have a P/E over 100 ($\log_{10}$ of P/E > 2). The line is the line of best fit: other things being equal, you would expect a company with a market capitalisation of £10m to have a P/E of 10.4. Since the logarithms are base 10, this company would be near point (1,1) in the scatter plot. On the other hand, there are three giant companies (circled) with market capitalisations close to £100bn, or $£10^{5}$m. According to the line of best fit you would expect these to have P/Es of 21.3, but in fact they have relatively low P/Es for their size, of 9.9 (HSBC), 6.3 (BP) and 11.3 (Vodafone).

Companies in particularly exciting high-growth sectors can also have very high P/Es of 20, 25 or more, even when there is no market bubble in operation. This is because of that future growth: if you are confident that a company will be growing strongly for years to come, then you should be prepared to pay a higher price now for a share of that growth. The high P/E is justifiable, *provided* that the expectation of long-term high growth turns out to be correct.

# Historical and prospective P/E

Historical and prospective P/Es are calculated on the basis of the historical and prospective EPS:

$$\text{historical P/E} = \frac{\text{yesterday's closing share price}}{\text{historical earnings per share}}$$

Thus if a company earned 3p per share according to the most recent annual report and the share price closed at 24p yesterday, then the shares cost eight times a single year's earnings and the company has a historical P/E of 8 (sometimes written as '8x').

This is the most widely quoted figure, and the one that will be used in any academic research into how well P/Es predict share price returns, but it can be seriously out of date. In the worst case, the preliminary results for the company year just ended might be about to come out (and 120 days of grace are allowed before preliminary results must be published), but the EPS quoted is still that from the *previous* company year. So the historical P/E could be based on some items sold and costs incurred up to two years and four months ago.

A more up-to-date but less reliable P/E is the **prospective P/E**:

$$\text{prospective P/E} = \frac{\text{yesterday's closing share price}}{\text{prospective earnings per share}}$$

This is more up to date than the historical P/E because it is based on earnings expected by analysts over the current company year, i.e. sales currently taking place and costs currently being incurred. However, it is less reliable because it is based on analysts' forecasts rather than accounting fact. Also, as explained in the previous chapter, the forecast EPS is only calculated if at least three analysts are following the company. Many small (sub-£50m market capitalisation) companies will likely only have their house analyst following them, and so do not have a prospective P/E. Historical back-tests of investment rules that want to use the full range of companies quoted on the stock market can therefore only use the possibly out-of-date historical P/E.

## Example

**Table 1: Inchcape and Haynes EPSs and P/Es, February 2012**

| | Historic | Forecast (current year) | Forecast (next year) |
|---|---|---|---|
| Inchcape price | 364p | 364p | 364p |
| Inchcape EPS | 32p | 34.81p | 37.53p |
| Inchcape P/E | $\frac{364}{32} = 11.4$ | $\frac{364}{34.81} = 10.5$ | $\frac{364}{37.53} = 9.7$ |
| Haynes price | 195p | 195p | 195p |
| Haynes EPS | 29p | - | - |
| Haynes P/E | $\frac{195}{29} = 6.7$ | - | - |

Table 1 shows the different P/Es that can result. Inchcape's earnings forecasts rise steadily over the next two years, so the P/E drops gradually. Haynes with a market capitalisation of £19m does not have enough analysts following it to have a prospective P/E quoted, so has only its historic P/E of 6.7.

## Earnings yield and the E/P

Earnings yield is simply the inverse of the P/E, expressed in percentage terms. It gives a figure analogous to the bond yield, except for the fact that the earnings go initially to the company, not the investor. (Dividend yield is more closely analogous, since the shareholder actually receives the dividends.)

If one share costing 24p gave 3p EPS:

$$\text{earnings yield} = \frac{3}{24} \times 100\% = 12.5\%$$

The earnings yield (without the percentage format) is universally used instead of the P/E in academic research. There it is referred to as the E/P. This is not just because finance researchers love technical jargon: the P/E has a nasty discontinuity in it. A share price can never go to precisely zero but EPS can, so you want EPS as the numerator, not the denominator. Consider a company with a share price of £10 that made +0.1p EPS last year:

$$\frac{P}{E} = \frac{1000}{0.1} = 10000; \quad \frac{E}{P} = \frac{0.1}{1000} = 0.0001$$

If the same company makes just a few pounds less and hence a 0.1p EPS loss:

$$\frac{P}{E} = \frac{1000}{-0.1} = -10000; \quad \frac{E}{P} = \frac{-0.1}{1000} = -0.0001$$

The P/E has gone through a discontinuity as the EPS passes through zero when the E/P has not. This is likely to cause problems when assigning companies to portfolios based on their P/Es, hence the E/P is used instead. Many studies in fact exclude loss-making companies altogether: although a (negative) P/E can be calculated if a company makes a loss, it is intuitively difficult to think what a negative P/E means.

# Chapter 4
**Practical Calculation of EPS and the P/E from Company Accounts**

We have now covered in detail the theory of how EPS and the P/E are calculated. Now we can put this into practice using a real-life example: Haynes Publishing, publishers of the famous motor manuals. For the sake of this exercise I shall evaluate the company in mid-2011 when its share price was 255p.

# Profit

Haynes' profit last year can be found in its latest annual report, available from the investor section of its website **www.haynes.co.uk**.

**Figure 3: Extract of Haynes' company report – profit and loss account**

### Consolidated Income Statement
Year ended 31 May 2011

| | | 2011 £000 | 2010 £000 |
|---|---|---|---|
| | **Continuing operations** | | |
| Note 2 | **Revenue** | **32,743** | 33,310 |
| | Cost of sales | (11,937) | (11,910) |
| | **Gross profit** | **20,806** | 21,400 |
| | Other operating income | 214 | 325 |
| | Distribution costs | (7,007) | (7,926) |
| | Administrative expenses | (6,326) | (6,113) |
| Note 4 | **Operating profit** | **7,687** | 7,686 |
| Note 6 | Finance income | 1,283 | 1,053 |
| Note 7 | Finance costs | (1,793) | (1,571) |
| | **Profit before taxation from continuing operations** | **7,177** | 7,168 |
| Note 8 | Taxation | (2,428) | (2,486) |
| | **Profit for the period from continuing operations** | **4,749** | 4,682 |
| | Attributable to : | | |
| | Equity holders of the Company | 4,742 | 4,677 |
| | Non-controlling interests | 7 | 5 |
| | | **4,749** | 4,682 |
| Note 9 | **Earnings per 20p share** | Pence | Pence |
| | Earnings per share from continuing operations | | |
| | – Basic | 29.0 | 28.6 |
| | – Diluted | 29.0 | 28.6 |

The top line of the income statement is revenue, i.e. Haynes' total revenue from publishing from 1 June 2010 to 31 May 2011.

As we saw in the previous chapter, as we move down the income statement more and more costs are deducted, starting with cost of sales and followed by distribution and administrative costs. Further details of these costs are given in the notes to the accounts. This gives operating profit of £7,687,000. Finance costs (loan interest) are then set against finance income (interest earned on cash and investments) to give profit before tax of £7,177,000. Finally tax is deducted, to give profit after tax of £4,749,000. This remaining profit is that attributable to shareholders (non-controlling interests represent the portion of profits in subsidiaries that is not held by Haynes Publishing Group). It is the £4,742,000 of profit attributable to equity holders of the company that is used to calculate the EPS figure used in the P/E ratio.

## EPS

We now divide the profit attributable to shareholders by the number of shares to get the historic EPS:

$$\text{EPS} = \frac{\text{profit attr. to shareholders}}{\text{weighted avg. no. of shares in issue}} = \frac{£4,742,000}{16,351,540} = £0.29$$

A weighted average has to be used because companies often issue more shares during the year as part of their executive bonus scheme. This increases the number of shares in issue and so dilutes the earnings attributable to each existing share. Large-scale fund-raising by issuing more shares is much rarer.

In fact Haynes did not issue any shares in 2011, so the weighted average is the same as the number of shares at the end of the financial year. Haynes also spares us another complication, diluted earnings per share, as there are no options outstanding to executives or employees. Haynes' diluted EPS is 29p, the same as its basic EPS.

The company has in fact already done this calculation for us in the bottom lines of the income statement. Haynes' EPS is 29p, but we can check the basis of the calculation in Note 9 to the accounts:

**Figure 4: Extract of Haynes' company report – earnings per share**

Earnings per share

The calculation of the basic and diluted earnings per share is based on the following data:

|  | 2011 £000 | 2010 £000 |
|---|---|---|
| **Earnings:** | | |
| Profit after tax - continuing operations* | 4,742 | 4,677 |
| **Number of shares:** | | |
| Weighted average number of shares (note 20) | 16,351,540 | 16,351,540 |

* Figure has been adjusted to exclude a profit of £7,000 (2010: £5,000) attributable to non-controlling interests.

As at 31 May 2011 and 31 May 2010 there were no outstanding options on either of the Company's two classes of shares and there is no difference between the earnings used in the basic and diluted earnings per share calculation.

# The P/E

We can now divide the share price by the EPS to calculate the P/E ratio. In early 2012, therefore, Haynes' P/E ratio is:

$$P/E = \frac{price}{earnings\ per\ share} = \frac{195p}{29p} = 6.7$$

In other words, an investment of 195p per share costs about seven times earnings per share. This is on the low side, even for a small company, but it is still fairly near the centre of the cloud in Figure 2.

# PART II
## The Value Premium and the P/E

In Part I we learnt the basics of what the P/E is and how it became popular during the 20<sup>th</sup> century. In this Part we move on to the much more contentious area of how it is used today.

Strangely, when the P/E became popular in the 1920s in the US, there was no statistical evidence that low P/E companies would give you better returns. There was of course the idea that for a P/E of 10 you are paying £1 for every 10p of annual earnings, and for a P/E of 20 you are paying £2 for those same earnings. You would therefore expect high P/E stocks to have better prospects for future earnings growth. Without this, if your investment prospects were in a steady state with no particular future growth expected, then it would make sense to pay the lowest P/E possible. Other things (most importantly, dividends) being equal – why pay £2 for 10p of earnings when you could pay £1?

It was only in 1960 that anyone suggested that low P/E stocks *as a class* will tend to give better long-run returns. This is what the 'value premium' means: value stocks, identified by having a low P/E, outperform glamour (high P/E) stocks. As we shall see in Chapter 5, the P/E is only one of the ratios you could use to identify such stocks.

As the idea came from an investment practitioner, not a finance academic, it was not rigorously tested for some years. What's more, the whole idea of markets being efficient was just getting started in the 1960s. If markets are efficient and stocks are efficiently priced then it should not be possible consistently to beat the market, whatever investment rule you follow. The mere suggestion that any particular class of stocks could consistently outperform the rest was unwelcome, particularly coming from an outsider.

Nevertheless, the findings have been backed up by hundreds of academic papers over many differing time periods and countries: over the long-term and on average, a portfolio of low P/E stocks will outperform the average of the market by around 3% p.a., and high P/E stocks will underperform it by the same margin. I am unaware of *any* paper that reports the opposite, i.e. that high P/E stocks outperform, at least over any long time period of a decade or more.

The outstanding argument is over whether these outperforming low P/E stocks are in some way riskier. Nobody should be able to get a free lunch of higher returns without some drawback, and the natural response is that low P/E stocks must be riskier in some way to account for those superior returns. Other studies have suggested ways in which this riskiness might make itself apparent, but there is no general agreement.

Many investors believe, on the basis of this evidence, that a company having a low P/E is a good sign for future returns. The P/E is just one of the ratios that these 'value investors' use to identify their stocks. On the other hand are those who believe that the market is in general an efficient place and that such stocks would have been snapped up long ago. (There is also plenty of evidence to back up their view that the market is by and large efficient.) According to these people, if you buy low P/E stocks (or any other company identified by its ratios as a 'value stock') then you are probably just buying a pig in a poke: it deserves to be cheap and the market has marked it down. Your money would be better spent by investing in a tracker fund, and your time better spent by searching for a tracker fund that follows the market as closely as possible for the least cost.

This fundamental split between the philosophy of value investors and believers in market efficiency appears in the world of academic finance just as in the real world of investment.

In this Part I shall introduce what value companies are, what value investing is and some of the famous people who do it. We then have a detour into efficient markets theory and why this value premium is an offence against this traditional orthodoxy. I cover the evidence on the returns when you use the P/E to identify value companies and the risks involved, I hope without you feeling you might as well read an academic paper. I skip through some of the later papers that try to reconcile market efficiency and the value premium. Since all of these are looking at US shares, I finish by assessing how much all this is reflected in UK work.

# Chapter 5
## Value Investing

As anybody who has traded on the stock market for any period of time will tell you, the prices of shares seem to gyrate much more wildly than their usually stable series of dividend payments would suggest. This was quantified by economist Robert Shiller in 1981, who estimated that prices vary 13 times as much as you would expect based on the variability of their dividend payouts. Trying to explain this inconvenient fact was one of the spurs to the field of behavioural finance that has grown up since. Behavioural finance tries to apply ideas from psychology to explain some of the otherwise inexplicable things we observe in financial markets. Surely it should be possible to identify shares that are in an irrational downswing?

## What is a value share?

Value shares are shares that appear unusually (and, the buyer hopes, unreasonably and temporarily) cheap compared to some measure of the fundamental value of the company. Here are some of the measures that have been used over the years to try to identify undervaluation, together with the accounting statistic they are based on:

**Table 2: Ratios for identifying value and glamour shares**

| Measure | Ratio | Acronym | Expectation for a value share | Expectation for a glamour share |
|---|---|---|---|---|
| Earnings | Price-earnings ratio | P/E | Low | High |
| Book value of assets | Price to (tangible) book value | P[T]BV | Low | High |
| Cash flow | Price to cash flow | PCF | Low | High |
| Sales | Price to sales ratio | PSR | Low | High |
| Dividends | Dividend yield | DY | High | Low |

When looking at the assets a company has, many value investors use tangible assets only, so that their preferred ratio would be PTBV and not PBV. Intangible assets might be worth billions (e.g. Coca Cola's trademark) down to nothing (the billions a company paid in 2000 for that internet company with no physical assets, that was clearly more or less worthless a few years later but still has a couple of employees so is still on the books). It is very much a matter of opinion what intangible assets are actually worth. So a conservative valuation will use only assets that you can in principle touch. Even a debt that has probably gone bad could be sold at a discount to a debt collection company, and you could go down to the bank and get the money they paid you out of the cash machine. You can't physically touch the rights to Coca-Cola's trademark, however valuable they are.

Dividend yield is the odd one out in Table 2 because it is calculated the opposite way round to the others. The top four ratios are all price divided by the measure in the first column, but DY is the dividend divided by the price. For some reason no-one uses price divided by dividend paid, and nobody talks about the 'price–dividend ratio'. Possibly DY is popular because it can easily be compared to other yields such as the running yield on a bond or the interest paid on a savings account.

Value shares will have at least one investment ratio, and possibly all of them, conforming to the 'Expectation for a value share' column above – a low P/E or high DY for example. They will also usually be the sort of share that people are only likely to have heard of if they have had particular dealings with that company. The example used in this book, Haynes, is a typical value share in that they have a low P/E and you are only likely to know much about them if you are interested in repairing cars. Haynes don't appear in the financial press very often because they are not popular with investors, which is of course part of their attraction. Indifference leads to a low share price. Utility companies are also typical value shares – low P/Es, high dividend yields, and usually very boring. The trouble with value shares is that you are not likely to gain any respect at dinner parties for owning them and you will get a reputation as a bore if you try to talk about them.

Glamour shares are the opposite of value shares: exciting shares that people talk about at the sort of stylish dinner parties that I don't get invited to. In 2000 people were talking about technology and in particular internet companies. In the 1970s it was electronics. Back in the mid-19th century it was railway companies. More recently it has been mining companies that everyone has been talking about. Their investment statistics are at the opposite end of the scale to those of value shares. They may have P/Es of 20, 25 or more, and if they pay dividends at all, the dividend yield will be of the order of 1% or 2%.

As Warren Buffett says: "You pay a high price for a cheery consensus." There is incontrovertible academic evidence that glamour shares underperform the market, and value shares outperform it.

# The value premium

The value premium is more often mentioned as such in academic finance journals than in general books on investing, but it underpins the whole idea of value investing. If you hold a portfolio of value shares, over many years you should do better than the market average, and even better against a portfolio of glamour shares. This has been quantified fairly accurately: value shares outperform the market, on average over many years, by 3-4% per annum. Glamour shares underperform it by the same amount.

This does not happen every year. Indeed, glamour can quite easily outperform value for several years running, which can be a big problem for fund managers who want to follow a value strategy. If they underperform their benchmarks for even four quarters running, they are quite likely to find themselves out of a job, or at the very least find a worryingly large proportion of their investors withdrawing their money. From 1995 to 2000 glamour shares outperformed value in every year, but it is the long-term average over decades that we are talking about here.

The difference might not sound like much, but, as investment commentators always say, shares are for the long-term. As an example of the magic of compound interest, to get a long but fixed period let's take the 18 years of a Child Trust Fund (CTF), the UK government-funded savings account for children. The creation of new CTFs was one of the first things axed by the incoming coalition government in 2010 but the millions of CTFs created for children born since 2002 will continue. Using the long-term average figures for value and glamour shares quoted above, something like this will happen:

**Table 3: Terminal values of a £250 CTF after 18 years**

| Investment type | Assumed average compound return per annum | Terminal value after 18 years |
|---|---|---|
| Glamour shares | 4% | £506 |
| Tracker fund (average of the market) | 7% | £845 |
| Value shares | 10% | £1390 |

The CTF investing in value shares ended up being worth almost *three times* as much as the CTF investing in glamour shares. The 7% market average cannot of course be predicted. Actual market average returns over any 18-year period could be higher or lower than that. But over such a long period the value–glamour split is quite predictable.

For the even longer period over which a pension is invested, the difference is even more marked. Let's assume that a 25-year-old puts a one-off £1,000 into a Self Invested Personal Pension (SIPP). He is planning to retire at 65, so has 40 years of growth ahead of him:

**Table 4: Terminal values of £1,000 invested in a pension fund after 40 years**

| Investment type | Assumed average compound return per annum | Terminal value after 18 years |
|---|---|---|
| Glamour shares | 4% | £4,801 |
| Tracker fund (average of the market) | 7% | £14,974 |
| Value shares | 10% | £45,259 |

Over 40 years the difference is more than *ten times*. Very clearly, anyone investing their own money for a pension should, first, start as soon as possible to get those compound returns rolling in, and second, keep most of their money in shares, and in value shares at that.

You won't find any collective pension fund doing this. They are likely to have a balanced portfolio of bonds, stocks and property because their horizon is much shorter term. For a start they have payments to existing pensioners to worry about. The reliable income from bonds and property comes in handy to take care of those current liabilities.

Also, as with professional fund managers, long-term decisions can have unpleasant short-term consequences. Pension fund trustees who made the decision in 1995 to invest mainly in value shares would have found themselves out of a job long before value shares finally started beating glamour shares again as the 1999-2000 technology stock bubble burst. It is only when investing your own pension pot that you would have the freedom to take a radical decision and invest mainly in value shares.

# Value investors

I could write many pages about value investing and its practitioners, but this is a short book about the P/E. I shall therefore summarise the methods of a few of the best-known value investors. For full biographies you will need to look elsewhere, but for details of many of these investment strategies I strongly recommend *The Intelligent Investor* by Ben Graham (1949 but never out of print) and David Dreman's 2012 book *Contrarian Investment Strategies: The New Psychological Breakthrough*.

## Warren Buffett

There are a few famous investors who follow value investing ideas as a matter of philosophical principle. One such is Warren Buffett – the most famous value investor. His aphorisms are almost as famous as his enormous wealth. One of them is that when you first hear about value investing it either clicks in the first ten minutes, or you never get it. This does not mean that every value investor follows the same formula. Despite belonging to the same church, they all have different methods and would no doubt have chosen to buy different companies, even if they had been investing at the same time and place.

Buffett's investment management company, Berkshire Hathaway is one of America's biggest companies. Indeed he is probably the best-known investor in the world due to his fabulous wealth. For years he and his friend Bill Gates were the richest two men in the world, although both have now been overtaken by Carlos Slim. His strategy of 'buying good-quality companies outright at a fair price', and then holding them permanently, is rather different to traditional value investors who try to pay as little as possible. He also insists that the companies he buys enjoy a 'sustainable competitive advantage'. That advantage, a much-loved brand say, a better business model, or a new product, should enable the company to earn outsized profits for years, or decades to come. By favouring companies that are both highly profitable and highly predictable, Buffett has performed 'satisfactorily', as he puts it: over the 40 years from 1967 to 2007, Berkshire Hathaway's average returns were 24.7% per year.

In some ways Buffett's methods defy comparison with other investors. For example, Berkshire Hathaway owns many companies outright, including insurance companies that provide him with free finance. Buffett describes insurance as a "collect now, pay later" model because ultimately most of the premiums the insurance companies take in will be paid out in claims. In the meantime, they can invest the float, worth $69bn in 2009, and the return is profit for Berkshire Hathaway. Access to free money is not a luxury most investors have. Neither do they have Buffett's reputation, which attracts successful business people to sell him their businesses at reasonable prices, so that they can be a part of Berkshire Hathaway.

Unlike the next two investors I cover, Warren Buffett hasn't written any books on investment. There have been several books written about Buffett though, which try with varying success to pin down his investment strategy because he has never really spelled it out. There are also his annual letters to shareholders, which are available for free on the Berkshire Hathaway website. These are often a valuable read. For example, in his 2002 letter to shareholders he warned of derivatives as being financial weapons of mass destruction, long before the markets in CDOs, CDSs and the rest grew large enough to threaten the global financial system in 2008-9.

## Ben Graham

There is no doubt in Buffett's mind that his development as an investor started at Columbia University, where he studied under Ben Graham and his fellow teacher and co-author, David Dodd. Together they wrote *Security Analysis* in 1934, a textbook that remains widely read today (although because half of it concerns investing in bonds, it is probably more accurate to say that half of it remains widely read to this day). In the foreword to the sixth edition, Buffett wrote:

> "My intellectual odyssey ended, however, when I met Ben and Dave, first through their writings and then in person. They laid out a roadmap for investing that I have now been following for 57 years. There's been no reason to look for another."

Ben Graham towered over US investment history for much of the 20th century, as his protégé, Buffett, who went to work for Graham in the 1950s, has since. His other major work, *The Intelligent Investor* in 1949, is a marvel of precise writing and dry wit. For what it's worth, I agree with Warren Buffett that *The Intelligent Investor* is the best book on investing ever written.

Graham only bought shares if there was a considerable "margin of safety" between the price he was paying and what he thought the company was worth. He also made a clear distinction between what is investment and what is speculation.

"An investment operation is one which, upon thorough analysis, promises safety of principal and an adequate return. Operations not meeting these requirements are speculative."

Emotion should expressly be excluded from the analysis, he said. Businesslike investment activities should be influenced solely by the available statistics. The investor is neither right nor wrong because others agree or disagree with him; he is right because his facts and analysis are right.

The same logic applies to much popular debate on scientific issues today, such as that on climate change. Whether climate change scientists' predictions are right or wrong depends solely on whether their data are correct and their models realistic. It doesn't depend on some informal vote of 2000 scientists, the vast majority of whom know no more about the details of climate change models than you or I do. When somebody tells you that the scientific consensus supports his view, he is tacitly admitting that his view is less than watertight. Nobody needs to appeal to the scientific consensus on Einstein's theory of general relativity or the laws of quantum mechanics: they are simply right and all available tests confirm them.

Graham introduced the concept of the irrational 'Mr. Market'. Each day Mr. Market comes to you offering to buy or sell you shares. However, Mr. Market is a manic-depressive, and often offers to buy or sell the shares at inflated or depressed prices. It is up to you whether you wish to take advantage of his mood swings. If you refuse to trade Mr. Market will always be back the next day regardless. With this idea Graham pre-empted the work of the behavioural finance professors now trying to explain the market's wild vicissitudes. In his forensic examination of company accounts, he inspired the next generation of value investors. At the dawn of the computer age he showed another generation of stock pickers how they could screen the market for companies meeting simple investment criteria and assemble portfolios that would handsomely beat the market average.

## David Dreman

One of that generation was David Dreman, who is primarily a professional fund manager. His firm, Dreman Value Management, ran $4.4bn in funds in early 2012. It offers a variety of low P/E value/contrarian strategies, both as collective funds and to individual wealthy investors.

Dreman has also written several books – most recently, *Contrarian Investment Strategies: The New Psychological Breakthrough* in 2012. This is an excellent read, although I hope Dreman would not mind me saying that his writing style is not up to Ben Graham's standard (and neither is my own). The book gives full details of the behavioural biases that lead to value opportunities, a summary of the academic evidence for and against efficient markets, and has several examples of Dreman's favoured investment strategies. Many of them are P/E-based but he also looks at using the other value indicators detailed in Table 2. Dreman shows how you can combine these value indicators with company size filters, e.g. investing only in large or small companies, or investing in particular industries. You can end with complex two- (or higher-) dimensional filters so that, for example, you only buy low P/E stocks in industries that themselves have high PEs. The problem with these is that there is any number of combinations of filters and only a small number of them have ever been tested.

Dreman's use of the term 'contrarian investing' rather than 'value investing' should be mentioned. He uses contrarian investing to mean buying depressed stocks that no-one else is interested in that nevertheless have good underlying statistics such as a low P/E. Dreman thus means more or less what Part II of this book is about.

Another meaning of contrarian would see it as buying a stock *solely* because it has dropped, say, 99% in the last year, without troubling to make any calculation of the company's true worth. This approach has scant academic evidence in its favour, and, following Ben Graham, there is no reason why it should have. You would be neither right nor wrong to buy such a share just because everyone else had voted it down. You would need to look at the other statistical evidence.

## Anthony Bolton

Well-known value investors in the UK are rather scarce. However, one of the best-known and longest serving fund managers is Anthony Bolton. He ran the Fidelity Special Situations Fund from its launch in 1979. Although he stepped down from day-to-day running of the fund in 2007, Bolton multiplied investors' money 147 times between its launch in 1979 and 2007, at an average annual rate of 19.5%. In 2010 he moved to Hong Kong to run a special situations trust investing in China.

Bolton's approach should be familiar by now: find undervalued companies which are currently out of favour with the majority of investors, but which are likely to come back into favour over a one- to two-year time span. Unlike many value investors, Bolton was very widely diversified, with his fund holding up to 200 companies. There are about 1300 companies excluding investment trusts quoted in London, so this is well over one-tenth of the market. Because he never followed an index, Bolton's returns were volatile, but he kept his job thanks to his outstanding long-term performance. As he observed, you can only hope to outperform the market if you don't hold the market portfolio.

One other point Bolton emphasised was not being over-impressed by managers. Bolton's opinion was that managers who interview well, and can answer analysts' questions convincingly, are not necessarily those who will perform well at the altogether more difficult tasks of running a company day-to-day and growing its profits in the long-term. This is rather at odds with Warren Buffett, who always gets to know the management of a possible Berkshire Hathaway purchase personally and only buys the company if the CEO is the sort of man he would consider as a possible son-in-law. There is obviously more than one way to be a successful value investor.

## The P/E value premium: early years

Since this book is about the price–earnings ratio rather than value investing in general, let's now cover the value premium as it applies to the P/E in detail.

That low P/E companies tend to outperform high P/E ones was in fact the earliest value premium to be demonstrated, even though it has fallen out of favour somewhat in recent years. In a three-page paper in 1960, a bank trust investment manager in Philadelphia called S. Francis Nicholson, working without the benefit of computers, retrospectively took 100 stocks and held groups sorted by the P/E as portfolios. He did this repeatedly over four five-year periods, from 1939 to 1959. The one-fifth of companies with the lowest P/E would have delivered an investor 14.7 times his or her original investment at the end of the twenty years, as compared to 4.7 times for the highest P/E stocks.

Nicholson suggested that, although glamour stocks may merit high P/E ratios, often prices have risen faster than earnings. For particular exceptional stocks, the price action continues spectacularly, and it is these exceptional stocks that cause the public to see high P/E ratios generally as evidence of further potential explosive growth and price appreciation. Eventually, reality makes itself felt and it is at this stage that high P/E stocks give poor returns. Nicholson was proposing what psychologists and behavioural finance researchers now call the availability heuristic, years before it was described as such. This is the reason why people are much more afraid of plane or train crashes than car crashes, even though car crashes kill many more people. It is the more extreme events that stick in one's memory.

There was little reaction from the growing world of academic finance. There were two other papers, one of which backed up Nicholson and one of which criticised his survivorship bias. He had only included firms that still existed in 1960, thus overestimating returns because he didn't include firms that went bust while he was holding them. In the mid- to late 1960s belief in efficient markets was taking hold, and someone who wasn't even a finance academic suggesting that some sets of stocks performed better than others was unwelcome.

Nevertheless, Nicholson persisted and wrote another paper in 1968. He was now retired but had access to his former employer's computer facilities for the first time. This time he looked at almost 200 companies from 1937 to 1962, and checked for whether the price-to-sales ratio and price-to-book value ratios worked the same as the P/E. You can see Nicholson's results over seven year holding periods in Table 5.

**Table 5: Seven-year returns grouping by P/E, price-to-sales ratio and price-to-book value, from Nicholson (1968)**

| P/E | Average growth over 7 years | Price to sales | Average growth over 7 years | Price to book value | Average growth over 7 years |
|---|---|---|---|---|---|
| < 10 | 131% | > 5 | 138% | > 1.5 | 149% |
| 10-12 | 87% | 2-5 | 108% | 1-1.5 | 112% |
| 12-15 | 88% | 1-2 | 107% | 0.6-1 | 91% |
| 15-20 | 75% | 0.6-1 | 89% | 0.3-0.6 | 90% |
| > 20 | 71% | < 0.6 | 69% | < 0.3 | 86% |

Whatever measure of company value he used, Nicholson got similar results: the lower the value group, the better the returns. He also tried sorting stocks in two dimensions, which is another trick that has only become widespread much more recently. Companies with, say, low P/E *and* low price-to-book value gave even better returns. Nicholson sensibly concluded:

> The purchaser of common stocks may logically seek the greater productivity represented by stocks with low rather than high price–earnings ratios.

Being a practical investor (many academic finance researchers have never owned a share, seeing it more as some kind of intellectual game[2]), he went on to criticise analysts' reports that quote P/E ratios of 20 or 50 with no comment as if they are normal. Nicholson saw it as vital to show common sense and relate business data such as assets, sales and depreciation to the current price.

I should emphasise that there is no longer any academic argument about the fact that value shares outperform. There have been hundreds of studies over the years, using different methodologies, in different countries with different data periods. Pretty well without exception they point the same way: value shares (with all the various different ways you can identify them) give better returns in the long run than the average of the market, which in turn beats glamour shares. The argument is whether the outperformance of value shares is down to some element of risk that has not been fully allowed for, or whether value share investing really is simply a better deal. For example, if a sudden recession hits, maybe value shares perform particularly badly.

But the value premium is a problem for finance academics because it appears to show that one particular set of stocks, however you define value stocks, outperforms the market quite reliably in the long term. This is an offence against the theory of efficient markets.

---

[2] Alternatively, they may either be too poor or may see the stock market as a complete lottery.

# Chapter 6
**Efficient Markets and the CAPM**

'Been there, done that', any reader who has done a university corporate finance course may say, and move on with an involuntary shudder to the next section. A survey of developments in the world of academic finance is not what you might expect in a book on the P/E and how to use it (at least one that wants to sell a few copies). For any reader who hasn't done a corporate finance course, I should warn that this is very much a high-level overview of efficient markets theory. Those who find this section particularly compelling (it takes all sorts) will find a much more comprehensive treatment in any well-known corporate finance textbook.

Nevertheless a brief overview of the academic background really is needed. Without it you might understand what the value premium is but not why it is an anomaly. So, for those readers who have not had the dubious benefit[3] of taking a university corporate finance course, here, in a few paragraphs, is a summary of decades of work by academic finance researchers into how asset prices are set.

If you are already familiar with all of this and decide to skim over the rest of this chapter, please go forward with the main point: if markets really are efficient and correctly adjust to reflect all news as soon as it comes out, then any amount of analysis you do is useless. More highly trained, more knowledgeable analysts than you will ever be have already done it and the sum of all their work is already reflected in the market price. To get the best risk/return ratio you should buy and hold an index tracker fund that holds, in effect, the average of all the stocks on the market. Your time would be better spent searching out the tracker fund with the lowest charges, investing in it and then watching TV. So why are you reading this book?

## Efficient markets

Eugene Fama first proposed the efficient market hypothesis in 1970. Fama is the best-known finance academic in the world and has been producing finance papers in leading academic journals for 45 years. We shall be coming across some more of his work later. Rather like Bach, it is scarcely believable that one person could have produced so much top-quality output in one lifetime. In his 1970 paper, Fama suggested three different levels of market efficiency, which we need not go into here.

---

[3] In the sense of it being very doubtful whether having done such a course will make you a better investor, but it could quite conceivably make you a worse one.

The basic idea is that an efficient stock market must incorporate any news items quickly into its view of how much each company is worth. This is the Efficient Markets Hypothesis (EMH).

What do we mean by these 'news items' that need to be incorporated? Not all news moves markets. The sort of news that analysts and market-makers are interested in is news that changes investors' expectations of the profits a company might make in the future. If the company has just published its accounts, and they show a higher profit for the year than expected, that will influence investors' expectations. A prime example of news that will result in a price change is the announcement of a takeover bid. Takeover bids offer investors a fairly immediate profit that is readily quantifiable and therefore tend to result in immediate price changes.

A diagram should make this clear. In Figure 5 some good news about the company comes out at point A. This is a large company that has many analysts following it. The price moves immediately to a new higher level, and stays there (more or less). This is how an efficient market in a stock is supposed to work: dozens of analysts have incorporated the news into their spreadsheets of the company's worth, and the wisdom of the market has quickly settled to a new equilibrium price.

**Figure 5: Efficient and not-so-efficient markets**

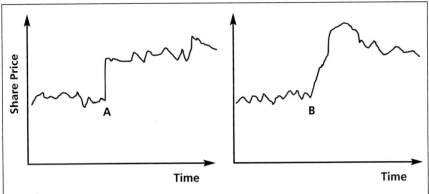

At point B in Figure 5, some good news comes out but the market is inefficient: it takes time to adjust, during which an alert operator could have bought into the trend. There was also clearly an overreaction, as the stock price trailed downwards afterwards. You will often get this (at least the slow adjustment part) with small stocks quoted on the main market or those on AIM. Trading volumes are of the order of a few thousand shares a day, and some days none are traded at all, compared to the tens or hundreds of millions of shares you would see traded daily for a FTSE 100 stock. Thinly traded companies can easily take several days to find a new equilibrium price, as the handful of private individuals who follow that share read the news and decide whether to buy or sell. It just isn't worth the time of the big boys to monitor such shares, so this is where a small private investor can hope to make a profit.

Note that the anomaly in B is the sort that will last a few hours or days. It is not the type of long-term value anomaly that this book is about exploiting. It is only there as an example of how markets might not be efficient for smaller companies, even for fairly obvious price-altering news in the short-term. In fact the biggest opportunities seem to come from companies and sectors systematically overlooked by investors. Such anomalies seem to last much longer. This is why value investors must be more patient and the value effect for an individual share can persist over, say, five years.

## The Capital Asset Pricing Model (CAPM)

The other major plank in efficient markets theory is the CAPM. Proposed by Bill Sharpe in 1964, it has shaped thinking on how markets value risky assets for two generations. He eventually won the Nobel Prize for Economics in 1990. (It seems that whether you win the Nobel Prize depends at least as much on your longevity as your contribution to human knowledge.)

Sharpe's insight was simple and seemingly undeniable: you should expect higher returns from riskier assets. He started with a series of simplifying assumptions (listed below) that made his market the mathematical equivalent of Fama's perfect efficiency. Some of his assumptions were eminently reasonable, but some of them were quite heroic and therefore may not be a fair description of the real world, to put it mildly.

1. Perfect competition (all investors are small and have to accept the prices they are given, i.e. no oligopoly).

2. All investors share identical time horizons (e.g. everyone is investing over one year only).

3.  Everyone can borrow or lend any amount at the risk-free rate.

4.  There are no taxes or transaction costs.

5.  All investors are rational mean-variance optimisers using the Markowitz portfolio selection model (basically they want to maximise returns but are also worried about risk).

6.  Homogeneous expectations (everyone recognises that future dividend payments are uncertain, but they all agree on what the different possibilities are and their probabilities).

Clearly some of these are more or less true. The model's predictions aren't much changed if you assume that taxes and transaction costs are there but small. Others are huge leaps of faith though. Investors have wildly different time horizons, from a day trader to a young worker putting money into a pension that will start to pay out in 40 years' time.

Once you swallow Sharpe's assumptions, however, it is all plain sailing, if not quite simple. What Sharpe accomplished back in 1964 is a mathematical *tour de force*. Sharpe was able to show that the expected return on a share, or any other risky asset, should be equal to what you could have got from gilts (the risk-free asset in the UK), plus a payoff related to the extra risk you are taking on. This payoff is the product of two factors:

1.  The stock's beta
    Beta is the name for the sensitivity of a company's share price to movements in the whole market. A stock with a beta of two tends to move twice as far as the market, so if the market goes up 10%, the stock should rise 20%. As with many smaller companies, Haynes is not much affected by stock market moves and has a beta of 0.52. Thus if the stock market rises 10%, it should rise 5.2%.

2.  The risk premium
    What shares return over gilts in the very long term (e.g. 100 years). Gilts are assumed to be risk-free in the UK context because the British government can if necessary raise taxes or print money to honour its obligations.

The consequences of believing in the CAPM and efficient markets are quite radical: no stock can be underpriced or overpriced for very long. (*How* long is unclear in the original CAPM, as it is a single time period model.) In the long term, all stocks must be priced according to the risk-free rate, their individual betas and the risk premium. Arbitrage is the mechanism by which prices move back into line, reflecting the balance between risk and reward. When investors see that a share is cheaper than it should be they buy it, pushing the price up; when they see a share that is more expensive than it should be, they sell it or short it, driving the price down.

The good news from the CAPM for researchers is that it provides a scientific model of the world that can be disproven. Like finding some electronic gadget in a stratum of dinosaur bones, one single piece of definite contrary evidence will disprove the whole idea. If *any* particular type of stock can be shown consistently to show better or worse returns than another type (for example, high- versus low-P/E stocks) then the ideas of efficient markets and/or the CAPM lie in doubt.

## Arbitrage Pricing Theory (APT)

The same cannot be said for the other model that we should cover briefly. The APT was originally proposed by Stephen Ross in 1976. Ross's insight is that there are many sources of risk for a stock, not just how much the stock moves relative to the market. As well as the risk-free rate, the same as in the CAPM, the expected return for any stock should depend on each of these risk factors, multiplied by how sensitive that stock is to that risk factor.

The risk factors aren't defined in Ross's original theory. Later papers have tested particular sets of risk factors, with varying results. The obvious risk factors to use are unexpected changes to inflation, Gross National Product (GNP), the interest rate, or any other economy-wide risk that could impact on particular stocks. Obviously some stocks are more sensitive to particular risk factors than others. This is why each stock has a different sensitivity to each risk factor.

All this sounds very reasonable and a useful way at looking at the riskiness of stocks. The problem with the APT is precisely its generality. The APT *as a whole* cannot be refuted. Only particular sets of risk factors can. You might run tests that show it does not work with your particular set of risk factors, but supporters of the APT can simply say that you were testing the wrong set of risk factors. The APT idea as a whole is not science, because it can never be disproven.

It cannot be over-emphasised to what an extent efficient markets, the CAPM, the APT and associated models (there have been several related ones since) have controlled the thinking of academic finance researchers over the years. Particularly in the 1970s and 1980s, any academic suggesting that the market wasn't really very efficient, or that the CAPM really wasn't a very good model for how the market prices stocks, would have great difficulty getting published. Any contrary evidence, that for example small stocks appear to give better returns than you would expect under the CAPM, was dismissed as the result of survivorship bias, or data mining, or with the comment that the researcher had obviously not considered all the possible sources of risk.

David Dreman in *Contrarian Investment Strategies: The Next Generation* writes of his difficulties getting his papers published. They weren't accepted or rejected. They were just left in a purgatory designed for papers that didn't fit the existing paradigm. It is only in the 1990s and 2000s that some senior voices in the world of academic finance have started saying that the emperor has no clothes. The debate continues as to whether the outperformance of particular types of stock (such as value stocks) is a *true* outperformance that offends against efficient markets, or simply an *apparent* outperformance that would disappear if the researcher were to consider all the possible sources of risk. This is excellent news for the continued employment of finance researchers, if not much use to anybody else.

## Reconciling efficient markets and the value premium

Recall that, at the end of Chapter 5, we covered S. Francis Nicholson's 1960 and 1968 papers that seemed to show particular types of stocks (among them lower P/E stocks) giving better returns than other types of stocks (among them high P/E stocks). Although Nicholson's research seemed to confirm the expectations of value investors and contradict EMH and the CAPM, it was another seven years before a 'respectable' finance academic, rather than an investment practitioner with metaphorical dirt under his nails, looked at the value premium.

Sanjoy Basu's papers in 1975 and 1977 confirmed Nicholson's results. He solved the survivorship bias by including a file of delisted shares so as to represent those shares actually trading on the market at the time at which he formed his portfolios, and this is now standard practice in any academic paper. Each 1 April over 14 years, Basu ranked stocks by P/E, grouped them into five portfolios each of one-fifth of the market (a quintile) and calculated the one-year returns for each portfolio. Since the CAPM beta calculations were by then common, Basu also tried to decide whether risk could explain the difference in performance. The results are shown in Table 6.

**Table 6: Annual returns and betas from Basu (1977)**

| P/E quintile | Average return p.a. | Beta |
|---|---|---|
| A (highest P/E) | 9.3% | 1.11 |
| B | 9.3% | 1.04 |
| C | 11.7% | 0.97 |
| D | 13.6% | 0.94 |
| E (lowest P/E) | 16.3% | 0.99 |

That returns increase as you move from group A to group E is very clear. Contrary to the CAPM's predictions, beta seems to bring very little to the party: beta changes very little across the groups, and what change there is seems to be in the 'wrong' direction, i.e. lower P/E stocks also have lower betas.

Basu's concern for the extra riskiness of low P/E portfolios was taken further by Ray Ball in 1978. He wasn't talking only about low P/E stocks, but he saw the outperformance of particular groups of stocks as a statistical artefact that had to be explained. Information available in the public domain at little or zero cost should not be the basis for any strategy that outperforms long-term, Ball argued. After looking at various possible explanations, he suggested that at least part of the problem was down to the P/E acting as a proxy for other variables that had not been included in the model. Basically he was saying that the P/E should be excluded from any model because it was correlated to some true risk variable that hadn't been identified yet.

This isn't an idea that can be proved or disproved. David Dreman compared this perspective to the phlogiston theory of the eighteenth century. Phlogiston was an attempt to explain oxidation processes such as fire and rust. Phlogiston theory saw metals not as elements, but as a combination of phlogiston with the metallic ore.

Phlogiston itself was a colourless and odourless liquid. Smelting expelled the phlogiston, and in combustion phlogiston left the combustible body to combine with or saturate air. It was basically moving in the opposite direction to how we now know oxygen atoms combine in combustion.

Disproving the existence of a colourless, odourless liquid was difficult. As with the APT, comprehensively disproving Ball's suggestion is impossible. You can include a host of possible sources of risk in your model, and quite possibly show that low P/E stocks aren't more risky according to any of them, but Ball and those who think like him can simply say that you missed something. Again, it's really not science.

One well-known paper did try to disprove Ball's argument: Fuller, Huberts and Levinson in 1993. They included a wide variety of possible explanatory factors for the outperformance of low P/E shares. They allowed for beta, industry classification and 13 other possible explanatory factors for risk such as earnings variability, leverage and foreign income. Again, they found higher returns for low P/E stocks, but the factors included in the model didn't explain those higher returns:

> *Unfortunately, neither earnings growth subsequent to forming E/P portfolios, nor analysts' forecast errors, nor omitted risk factors account for these abnormal returns. The E/P Effect remains an enigma.*

## Later years: the P/E sidelined

The P/E today might be as popular as ever in the mainstream investment industry, but among finance academics it has become a backwater. Finance researchers are concerned with trying to explain how stocks are priced and why value stocks give better returns on average, using complex multi-factor models on the same lines as Fuller, Huberts and Levinson. Basically, the P/E is heavily mixed up with a lot of other factors that may or may not predict returns better, depending on how the model is constructed and what factors you put into it.

For example, the fact that small companies show better returns in the long run has been known since a study by Marc Reinganum in 1981. Unfortunately, this small stock effect seems to come and go, as remarked on by Professors Elroy Dimson and Paul Marsh of London Business School in 1999. In fact it went into reverse once funds were established specifically to buy only small stocks. The further complication is that small stocks tend to have lower P/Es, at least in the UK. So whether the small stock effect turns out in your model as more important than the P/E effect depends not only on the factors you include in your model, but what time period and country your data are from.

Dissatisfaction with the original CAPM had been rumbling for years, due to the not inconsiderable fact that there seemed to be a whole lot of variation in returns that the theory couldn't account for. Value stocks were one of the apparent holes, small stocks another. Related models had been suggested to iron out some of the inconsistencies, such as the Consumption CAPM and the Intertemporal CAPM (if you want to find out about those, do a Finance MSc) but nothing really widely acceptable had been proposed until Eugene Fama again rode to the rescue.

# Chapter 7

**Accepting Reality: The Fama and French 3-Factor Model**

In a landmark series of papers in the early 1990s, Eugene Fama and his usual co-author Ken French changed the rules of the game. David Dreman unkindly described them as 'boldly thrusting thirty years into the past' because they seemed to be stealing some of the clothes of value investors. Fama and French (F&F) had already moved away from the simple CAPM position that beta can explain the differences in securities' returns. Now their papers proposed that company size and price-to-book value effects could explain stock returns. Under what soon became known as the Fama and French three-factor model, the expected returns for a stock in any one particular month depend on the risk-free rate plus:

1.   the market risk premium,

2.   a factor they called SMB (Small minus Big), to reflect the extra returns small stocks gave over big stocks in that month.

3.   a factor they called HML (High Minus Low [book value to market]), to reflect the extra returns that high book value to market value stocks gave that month, compared to low book value to market glamour stocks.

From Ken French's website, the market risk premium, SMB and HML for December 2011 were +0.86, -0.80 and +0.90 respectively. This means that for that month (only) the market gave 0.86% better returns than treasury bills, small stocks gave returns 0.80% worse than large stocks, and high book value to market stocks gave 0.90% better returns than low book value to market stocks. So the market risk premium was positive and stocks with a high book value compared to their stock market price also gave better returns. These are both as F&F's model proposes. However the 'small stock premium' worked in reverse that month: the shares of small companies gave worse returns than those of large companies. Note that these figures are for US stocks in that month alone, so you would need different factors to apply the F&F model to the UK. As far as I know no-one supplies these yet, and UK researchers have to calculate their own SMBs and HMLs if they want to apply the F&F model.

Given that the model included a value indicator in the form of book value to price, F&F claimed that any other value stock indicators such as the P/E were no longer significant. The three-factor model has been highly successful, and is now at least as widely used as the CAPM for modelling stock returns, but there are some important criticisms I want to mention.

## Are SMB and HML grounded in reality?

F&F explain the SMB and HML factors as being proxies for the riskiness of the stocks. They are saying that small stocks and high book value to price stocks are in some way more risky, and that is why they give higher returns. Arguably, this is valid for the sort of small companies traded on AIM in the UK that aren't followed by any analysts. They could have financial problems that aren't obvious from a superficial reading of their annual report, and anyway the reporting requirements aren't as strict as for companies with a full London Stock Exchange (LSE) listing. Small companies' fortunes will also often depend on the vagaries of one market sector, whereas large companies usually have divisions active in different sectors that can compensate for one another when times are hard for one division.

However, the idea that book value to price could be seen as a proxy for risk is distinctly questionable. A company with lowly rated assets might be in financial distress, or on the other hand it might be a very stable, low risk company such as a utility with few growth prospects. If you were asked to name an accounting statistic that might proxy for risk, book value to price would not be the obvious one you would choose.

Indeed, you might expect companies with high share prices relative to their book value to be in general more risky investments than those whose assets are lowly rated. Which would you think is more risky, a water company with a market capitalisation somewhat below the book value of its tangible assets, or a high-growth computer company with next to no tangible assets because its offices, computers and managers' cars are all leased? F&F say that the water company must be riskier to help explain the (on average) higher returns to be expected from its lower price to book value ratio. Describing book value to price as a risk factor seems something of a *post hoc* rationalisation.

Questioning whether HML is really a risk factor has parallels to the criticism Warren Buffett makes of beta in 'The Superinvestors of Graham and Doddsville' at the back of *The Intelligent Investor*. High prices are more risky and low prices are less risky, yet finance academics would think that a stock that had fallen a long way in comparison to the market is more risky. A respectable blue-chip stock costing £10 that drops 10p (1%) has shown minimal volatility. If the company has a run of bad luck and goes down to £1 it might well become interesting to value investors. If that stock at £1 then drops to 90p, the same 10p drop in price (now 10%) makes it much more volatile and hence riskier and less interesting to someone investing on the basis of the CAPM, but *more* interesting to a value investor. Warren Buffett has done rather well for himself despite not knowing the betas of his stocks.

## The F&F model is next to useless for real investors

Another important point to note is that these HML and SMB factors are complicated beasts. I won't go into the detail of F&F's calculations here, but the point to note is that each individual value for SMB and HML represents how much small stocks outperformed big stocks, or how much high book to value stocks outperformed low book to value stocks, *in that one month*. The model is therefore useless for investors who want to know what is going to happen even next month, let alone next year. It can only explain returns after the event. F&F suggested using average values for SMB and HML in any practical application, but if you have a look at the SMB and HML factors available for free from Ken French's website,[4] both factors vary considerably month to month. They can even remain 'the wrong way round' as far as value or small company investors are concerned for quite long periods.

## Lack of a theoretical underpinning

The CAPM, once you accepted its assumptions, was a logical mathematical development. You might argue with the assumptions, but you couldn't argue with Sharpe's mathematical logic: if you accepted his assumptions, beta was the *only* variable that should be capable of predicting returns. Crucially, unlike the CAPM, F&F have offered no theoretical underpinning as to *why* size and book value to price should be important factors in explaining returns, and not other factors. They simply showed that their factors were statistically a pretty good way of explaining the stock returns we have seen over the years. Convincing explanations are lacking to this day, and a minor industry has grown up in academic papers suggesting how the F&F factors might be improved or replaced.

---

[4] **http://mba.tuck.dartmouth.edu/pages/faculty/ken.french**

## The P/E in the F&F model

Finally, and importantly from the P/E's point of view, F&F tried to scotch in advance any suggestions that other value indictors might usefully be added to their model. The most likely candidates are the P/E and dividend yield, David Dreman's preferred statistics. F&F showed that neither the P/E nor dividend yield could add anything to their model, because it already contained a value share indicator in the form of price to book value.

*However*, their PBV was allowed to vary month by month, and the P/E and DY that they tested the model against didn't. They were supposed to have the same effect every month, but as we have seen, the value premium (or, in some months, the value discount) comes and goes over time.

Using F&F's own logic against them, with UK stocks I set up a model that already included a time-varying P/E factor and tested whether a non-time-varying PBV factor could add anything. It couldn't. F&F weren't testing the P/E on a level playing field with book value to price. In fact, tests on a level playing field, with neither factor allowed to vary by time, showed that book value to price *was* slightly better than the traditional P/E in the model, but that both were still significant predictors of returns. By enhancing the P/E, though (see Part III), it could be turned into a better value indicator than PBV.

# Chapter 8
## Value Investors Fight Back

I have looked at the F&F 3-factor model in much more detail than the CAPM or APT because it is the most widely accepted model of stock returns today, at least in the academic finance world. There are plenty of doubters who do not feel it explains everything however.

The best-known of these papers, Lakonishok, Shleifer and Vishny in 1994 (LSV), came out only one year after Fama and French's 1992 and 1993 papers. Given the time it takes to research a paper and get it published, it must have been in the pipeline before the F&F papers came out, rather than simply being a reaction to them. LSV's paper was an impressively comprehensive treatment of the subject of value versus glamour stocks. They looked at several ways of defining value for a value strategy: buying shares with low prices compared to some indicator of fundamental value such as earnings per share, book value per share, dividend paid per share or cash flow per share.

Another way was to look at past growth in sales and expected future growth as implied by the then-current P/E ratio. What they found was that the differences in expected future growth rates between value and glamour stocks seemed to be consistently overestimated by investors. Glamour stocks grew faster for the first couple of years but after that the growth rates of the two groups were basically the same. Value strategies using *both* past low growth and low current multiples outperformed glamour strategies by an impressive 10-11% per year.

Among the various measures of fundamental value, P/E did not produce as large an effect as price-to-book value or price-to-cash flow, possibly because-

> stocks with temporarily depressed earnings are lumped together with well-performing glamour stocks in the high expected growth/low E/P category. These stocks with depressed earnings do not experience the same degree of poor future stock performance as the glamour stocks, perhaps because they are less overpriced by the market.

In other words, the P/E didn't work as well as PBV at sorting out value stocks from glamour stocks because companies that had had one unlucky year ended up with minimal earnings. Say that bad weather one summer has caused an outdoor clothing chain, that had thin margins to begin with, a 90% drop in earnings. The share price hasn't dropped by anywhere near 90%, because everyone knows that bad weather is temporary. Since the P/E is the price divided by just last year's earnings, the company will have a high P/E and get lumped in with glamour stocks, not its more natural value stock brethren. When the weather gets better and the clothing chain's forecast earnings and share price improve, it pulls up the average returns of the whole basket of glamour stocks. It makes it look as if the P/E simply doesn't work very well.

This problem is solved by the long-term P/E described in Chapter 11.

LSV argued that value strategies provide higher returns because they exploit the irrational behaviour of investors. People assume that rapid growth in the past will translate reliably into rapid growth in the future. As we shall see in Chapter 10, earnings growth in the past is in fact an extremely poor indicator of earnings growth in the future. This is a very plausible explanation of why value outperforms: people overpay for growth.

Importantly for F&F's arguments about their SMB and HML factors being proxies for otherwise unobserved risk, LSV found 'little, if any' support for the view that value strategies were fundamentally riskier. Value stocks outperformed glamour stocks quite consistently and did particularly well in 'bad' states of the world.

## The P/E effect in the UK

So far we have only covered studies based on US data, because US studies are what everyone talks about. All the top finance journals are US-based. To put it bluntly, without using US data, unless your paper is Nobel Prize-level stuff, you are most unlikely to appear in the top finance journals.[5] Very few UK business schools can afford a subscription of several tens of thousands of dollars a year to the CRSP/Compustat US stock price database, which is what all the best studies are based on.

Nevertheless, there have been many studies that back up the US conclusions about the P/E. The first one in the UK was as late as 1989, by Mario Levis who is now a Professor at Cass Business School. Looking for evidence on value-based returns anomalies in the UK, he checked for returns from sorting stocks into portfolios based on company size, dividend yield and the P/E. Levis found clear effects for all three,

---

[5] And, of course, only professors who have published regularly in the top (US) journals are likely to be nominated for Nobel Prizes. Catch-22.

with the P/E giving for example 19.3% per annum compound returns for the lowest one-fifth of stocks sorting by P/E, compared to 13.2% for the market and 11.4% for the highest P/E quintile.

In 1997 F&F's three-factor model saw its first test outside the US, by Norman Strong at Manchester. The results were strongly supportive of the F&F model: the risk-free rate, the market risk premium, SMB and HML did an excellent job at explaining monthly returns here as in the US. As Fama and French found, the P/E was a marginally significant predictor of returns when tested on its own, but it lost its power when tested alongside book value to price.

A UK paper more supportive of LSV came out in 2001. Maria Michou at Exeter, with her PhD supervisors Alan Gregory and Richard Harris, followed LSV by testing not only one-way classification of stocks using the usual value indicators, but also two-way classification to group stocks that had shown poor past sales growth, so that they had apparently poor prospects. (But as with earnings, past sales growth or lack of it translates very poorly into a predictor for future sales growth.) Michou found that although the F&F three-factor model could explain the outperformance of value stocks under one-way classification, two-way classification defeated it.

Investing in stocks with both poor recent sales growth and poor prospects gave some really significant results – for example, an annual 12.53% difference between 'low sales growth/low PBV' and 'high sales growth/high PBV' portfolios. A follow-up paper by the same authors in 2003 tested whether the outperformance of value portfolios was due to unrecognised risk factors, as suggested by Ball back in 1978. They found no evidence that value stocks performed worse in bad states of the world, suggesting that they are not fundamentally riskier.

The UK is perhaps the country where the most studies have been done to test support for the US results. What is covered above are only a few of the most relevant papers. There have been literally hundreds of other studies around the world. All point towards supporting the results first found by Francis Nicholson in the US: value shares *do* outperform, and the effect is very robust with regards to which value indicator you use and which country you run the tests in. However, it is not very robust to the passage of time, at least over periods of a few years. It is only reliable if you average the performance over a decade or more. There can be even quite long periods when glamour outperforms value, which we saw most recently in the five-year run-up to the technology and internet stock bubble in 1999-2000.

What remains to be decided is whether value stocks really are somehow riskier, as F&F and their supporters maintain, or whether it is a true outperformance (perhaps because people assume that past growth is a more permanent feature than it really is) as LSV and *their* supporters claim. If this unwarranted projection of growth into the future really is the main cause of the outperformance of value stocks, that would make it one of the most important ideas in behavioural finance. The jury is still out on this question.

## Rehabilitating the P/E

From the very first paper in 1960, the P/E showed its promise for value investors. A low P/E *does* show companies that are going to outperform in the future, and this has been proven across different time frames and in different countries around the world. The remaining argument between academics is whether this really shows some basic inefficiency in the market, or whether the extra returns we see for low P/E stocks are merely rewards for accepting higher risk.

Far from being a useful but flawed value indicator, as Lakonishok *et al.* suggest, the P/E still has plenty of life left in it. Companies that had a bad year last year, showing wafer-thin earnings and thus a very high P/E, *can* be adjusted for. This is one of the subjects of Part III.

# PART III
# Improving the P/E

Given the P/E's long history, and the many people who use it every day, it is surprising that there have been very few attempts to improve it. The P/E is not some time-hallowed accounting measure such as asset turnover or return on capital employed. Most people who use the P/E are investors, trying to make their portfolios grow more quickly. They should be quite happy to have placed in their hands an improved version of the P/E that is more efficient at identifying companies that are going to outperform.

In this Part I first look at some developments of the P/E that are widely used by value investors. The P/E can be adjusted to take into account the market or industry P/E. One researcher has also suggested that you could take account of some earnings items in the accounts but not others. In Chapter 10 we move on to the PEG ratio. This is the best-known development of the P/E. It tries to adapt the P/E to make it more useful for very high P/E growth stocks, but it has some major problems, both at the technical and fundamental levels.

The remaining chapters in this Part look in detail at my own research on the P/E. All these ideas have previously been published in academic journals. However despite some interest when the papers came out they have not yet been taken up by professional fund managers or, if they have, they haven't told me. So you may get an advantage over professional investors having read this part of the book. The ideas covered here include:

- **The long-term P/E**: earnings, being the sometimes small difference between two large numbers (sales and costs), tend to be very volatile. Taking a longer-term view of earnings over the whole economic cycle gives a more reliable view of a company's earnings potential.

- **Decomposing the P/E**: there are many factors that affect a company's P/E that are not specific to the company itself. These include the overall market P/E, company size and the sector it operates in. Adjusting for these known influences improves the P/E's power.

- **The naked P/E**: after allowing for the regular influences above, there is something left over. Companies of the same size in the same sector always have different P/Es due to factors affecting only those particular companies. This unexplained part of the P/E turns out to be best at identifying the extreme ends of the value–glamour spectrum. It also turns out to be very risky when the stock market as a whole is doing badly.

# Chapter 9
## Developing the P/E

Here I cover three developments of the P/E that have become popular in recent years. The first two do not recalculate the P/E itself, but simply try to use it in a slightly more sophisticated way. The last one puts different numbers into the 'E' in the P/E calculation.

## The industry-adjusted P/E

Does the P/E effect work as well within industries? If I buy stocks with a P/E of 15 when the average for that industry is 20, should I expect to do as well as if I had bought stocks with a P/E of 8 when the industry's average is 13?

This is one of David Dreman's favourite strategies in his 1998 book. Sure enough, buying the lowest 20% of stocks by P/E in each industry showed a very similar outperformance over the long-term as simply buying low P/E stocks chosen from across the market. (As with other value strategies, the P/E is not unique here. The method worked equally well if he used dividend yield, price-to-book value or price-to-cash flow to identify value companies within sectors.) The lowest 20% of stocks in each industry gave 17.7% total returns from 1970 to 1996, compared to 12.2% for the highest P/E stocks from each industry. This is even though the low P/E group actually included some companies with quite high P/Es – they were just low for their industry.

Interestingly, Dreman suggests that investing across a range of industries will reduce your portfolio's overall risk, and help protect you in bad economic times. You no longer have to spend your life invested in utilities and manufacturing companies no-one has ever heard of if you use this strategy, and you will have something to talk about at dinner parties.

An example of someone who benefits from this industry P/E effect is Ed Owens of the Vanguard Health Care fund. As of February 2012 Owens' fund had a 16.3% compound annual return since its inception in 1984, widely outperforming the S&P 500 despite the fund's huge size of $21.4 billion. Although Health Care is usually thought to be a growth sector, Owens applies a long-term value approach to it. He disregards earnings disappointments and other temporary troubles, and considers what the market's attitude towards a company will be in a year's time. This results in a relatively stable portfolio. Owens' view is that acting contrary to how most investors are behaving gives him an advantage that does not show up in monthly or quarterly figures, but that makes itself felt in the long-term.

## The time-relative P/E

This is another well-known use of the P/E that does not involve transforming the statistic itself in any way. Here, we are simply comparing a company's P/E across time. If the company's P/E is a long way below what has been its long-term historical average, then that should be an indicator of value too, even if the P/E is not particularly low compared to the average of the market.

A good example of an investment manager who uses this approach is James Margard of Rainier Investment Management in Seattle. He uses previous years' earnings when he chooses stocks for his Core Equity Portfolio. This portfolio tries to maximise long-term capital growth by looking for companies with prospects of strong earnings growth but which are currently selling cheaply. This he refers to as GARP – Growth at a Reasonable Price.

Specifically, Margard takes the ratio of a stock's P/E compared to the market P/E in past years, and compares this to the ratio now. Margard is looking for this 'ratio of a ratio of a ratio' having a value considerably less than one. This should mean that the stock's P/E compared to the market is considerably lower than it was in previous years. Using this method, Margard should pick up growth stocks that have fallen out of favour recently, as well as the more usual value stocks.

## The P/E using operating income

Despite the P/E's popularity, there has been only one academic paper that looks at how the accounting values that go into the P/E calculation could be changed to make the P/E more useful to investors. (There is however also Joel Greenblatt's version of the P/E that I cover in Chapter 16.)

The 'P' part really isn't open to much reinterpretation. However, there is plenty that could be re-interpreted in the 'E' part of the P/E. In fact, as we saw in Chapter 2, exactly what items you put into the earnings denominator section of the P/E seems to have as many different definitions as there are data providers. Look up any company's current P/E from DataStream, Company REFs and the Companies section of the *Financial Times* and you will get three different answers. It doesn't help that different countries have different accounting procedures, and even within countries the definitions of what earnings and expenses fall above or below the line change over time.

Tony Kang in Singapore wrote a paper in 2003 looking at an alternative definition of earnings to see whether this would make the P/E of more use to investors. His suggestion was to use operating income. This appears a lot higher up the income statement than the basic or diluted EPS that is usually used. In particular it excludes taxes and finance costs.

Kang found that using operating income as the 'E' part of the P/E ratio worked considerably better at discriminating between value and glamour firms than the traditional P/E. Using US data on 19,000 US companies from 1982 to 1995, there was a much larger difference in returns between the top and bottom 10% of companies by P/E if he sorted them by a P/E that used operating income instead of the usual EPS, widening the difference in average annual returns between the top and bottom 10% of companies from 7.79% per year to 10.58%. Kang decided that the non-operating income component of earnings seemed to be very unpredictable, and this was what was reducing the P/E's power.

Having looked briefly at these simple refinements to the P/E, we will now look at one of the most popular variants of the P/E: the PEG.

# Chapter 10
## The PEG Ratio

Not many developments of the P/E ratio have become popular, despite the several decades that have gone by since use of the P/E became widespread. In fact the only development that has really caught on is the PEG ratio. This is a way of allowing for the fact that high-growth companies tend to have high P/Es. In the UK, Jim Slater's two popular *Zulu Principle* books are both largely based on using the PEG as a stock selection tool to throw up cheap growth stocks. Slater helped to design Hemmington Scott's Company REFS, which is one of the main information sources for UK private investors. PEGs are important there too, and your company only gets a PEG if (amongst other requirements) you can show a history of at least four years of positive and growing earnings.

## What is the PEG ratio?

PEG stands for PE/Growth. It's an attempt to account for the fact that you would expect companies that are growing quickly to have high P/E ratios. It is right and proper that companies with forecast long-term high growth should have higher P/E ratios. You are expecting higher earnings in the future, so it is only right that you should pay more for each pound of earnings in the present. The PEG is supposed to allow analysts who work in high-growth sectors to compare the P/E ratios of their companies, taking account of their growth potential, while still keeping the simplicity of a single multiple.

The formula for the PEG ratio is very simple:

$$\frac{\text{P/E ratio}}{\text{forecast EPS growth rate (\%)}}$$

So, for example, if you have a company with a one-year forecast P/E of 20, and the consensus among analysts is that it its EPS growth rate is 10% a year, then its PEG is 2.0.

Take the real-life example of Aggreko. They have EPS of 78.57p, one-year forecast EPS of 86.46p (growth of 10.2%) and two-year forecast EPS of 100.53p (growth of 16.3% on the one-year forecast EPS). Average forecast EPS growth over the two years is therefore 13.2%. A current P/E of 27.6 gives them a PEG of 2.09 (27.6/13.2), so their healthy forecast growth appears to be fully taken account of in their high current P/E.

The convention has grown up that a company is fairly valued if its PEG is close to 1.0, and if it's considerably below 1.0 then this could be a company worth spending some more time analysing. As Jim Slater says in *Beyond the Zulu Principle*:

> Shares with PEGs over one tend to be unappealing, shares with PEGs of about one are worthy of consideration and at well under one they are usually worth examining in much more detail with a view to purchase.

I write 'The convention has grown up' because there is a trap in the equation. The numerator and denominator are in different units. Dividing one by the other doesn't really make much sense. There's nothing stopping you dividing one by the other and getting a ratio, but the result won't necessarily mean very much. There is really no mathematical basis behind the idea that a fairly valued growth company should have a PEG ratio of 1.0.

Beyond this basic hole in the idea behind the PEG, there are big problems with the inputs into this equation. As computer programmers are fond of saying: garbage in, garbage out.

What P/E ratio do you use? As we saw in Chapter 3, you have a choice between the historic P/E and the consensus among analysts for what the P/E is going to be next year (the prospective P/E). Slater uses the prospective P/E.

What expected EPS growth rate do you use? Next year's growth rate, or the consensus expected growth rate averaged over the next five years? In fact as long as you use the same basis for all the PEGs you calculate, they will all be consistent.

How reliable are those growth estimates as statistics? Only the largest companies have a reasonable number of analysts making growth estimates. For companies that aren't in the FTSE 350 then you can basically forget about it. It just isn't worth analysts' time to study smaller companies. Even for FTSE 250 stocks you are likely to have less than ten growth rate estimates per company. Ten should be the absolute minimum for any statistically valid sample. And if you want to calculate the PEG ratio for a £50m technology company, you are going to be estimating its future growth rate on your own.

Most importantly, there is a deeper problem with earnings growth estimates. There is considerable academic evidence that earnings growth rates are *inherently not predictable*.

## Why can't we predict earnings growth rates?

The formula for the PEG implicitly assumes that we can reliably predict earnings growth rates over several years, i.e. that earnings growth rates vary only slowly. The assumption is that if a company has shown a high growth rate over recent years, then we can reasonably expect it to continue for some years to come, and cheerfully assign it a high P/E.

Only we can't, because they don't.

The unpredictability of the news flow in the real world seems to make a mockery of analysts' best efforts at predicting the future. Back in 1962, I.M.D. Little published 'Higgledy Piggledy Growth' in the *Bulletin* of the Oxford University Institute of Statistics. (There weren't any UK-based finance journals back then.) He took 400 companies over the previous 10 years, and tried to see how predictable their earnings growth had been with hindsight. This involved taking the fastest-growing 10% over the previous few years, then the next fastest-growing 10%, and so on, and seeing how that growth carried on into the future. If growth rates are predictable, then the 10% of companies growing fastest in the past should be among the fastest companies for growth in the future.

You can see one of Little's hand-drawn graphs below. Like Nicholson, Little obviously didn't have access to a computer then either.

**Figure 6: Subsequent growth after sorting firms into deciles based on prior growth, from Little (1962)**

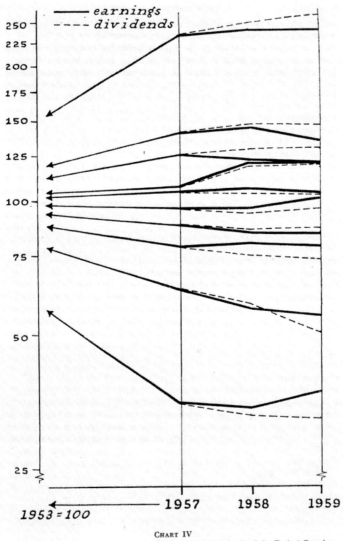

CHART IV

Indices of Subsequent Growth of Mean Earnings and Dividends of the Fastest Growing
Tenth, Second Tenth, and so on, of Large Firms in the Period 1953–57

The result is quite clear even from looking at the chart. Sorting firms by past earnings growth rates *didn't work*. He found 'little or no evidence for consistency in growth'. Basically, as soon as these portfolios of the 10% fastest-growing companies (or 10% slowest-growing companies, or whatever) were formed, they reverted immediately back to more or less the average growth rate for the market as a whole. Any difference in the growth rates after that were no more than you would expect by chance alone.

There have been several papers backing up Little's work since. Most recently, Josef Lakonishok (who co-wrote the LSV paper mentioned in Chapter 8) and others in 2003 did a major study covering every US company from 1951. They did find persistence in long-term growth rates, but only as much as you would expect by chance. Take 1000 people tossing coins in unison. After ten tosses, on average one person will have tossed a head every time. That doesn't mean that that person is more skilful at tossing heads, just lucky. The same applies to the handful of companies that have a consistent history of rapidly growing earnings.

Does that mean that the 'four years of positive and growing earnings' requirement in Company REFS for a company to be awarded a PEG is redundant?

## Testing the predictability of earnings in the UK market

I set up a database of all UK stocks from 1975-2004 and sorted them by how long their history of positive and growing earnings was. To see whether doing this was any use in predicting returns, I calculated the average returns over the next year for each group. Thus there was a successively more restrictive filter, from stocks showing only one year of positive earnings, to those showing a full eight years of positive and growing earnings. The results are shown in Table 7.

**Table 7: One-year average returns for stocks with a history of positive earnings, or of positive and growing earnings. All UK stocks, 1975-2004**

|  | History of positive earnings of... | History of positive and growing earnings of... |
|---|---|---|
| One year | 17.83% | 17.83% |
| Two years | 17.67% | 18.56% |
| Three years | 17.72% | 17.58% |
| Four years | 17.90% | 16.85% |
| Five years | 18.07% | 16.72% |
| Six years | 18.20% | 17.84% |
| Seven years | 18.27% | 17.41% |
| Eight years | 18.13% | 16.80% |

In the first row the 17.83% is the same in both columns, because there is no history of growing or falling earnings if you are only looking at last year's earnings. All companies that had positive earnings last year are represented in both columns. In the subsequent columns, the requirement for a company to appear becomes more and more restrictive. In the final row, all companies with a history of eight years of positive earnings (growing or not) averaged 18.13% returns over the next year. All companies with a history of eight years of positive earnings, *and growing earnings year by year,* averaged 16.8% returns over the next year.

Overall, the average returns do vary, but only slightly and not in any particular direction. Filtering your companies by the number of past years of positive earnings they can show, whether growing or not, does not appear to be an activity that will provide you with a list of companies that will give better returns. In other words, doing all this filtering would be a waste of time.

However, the same database showed that it is important to have *some* history of positive earnings. Companies with long histories of losses, or those that can't show any earnings history at all, unsurprisingly show poor returns and a much greater tendency to go bust. But once you have that all-important first year of profits, filtering stocks any further, by how long or how full of growth the earnings history is, makes very little difference to your returns thereafter.

## So what use is the PEG ratio?

If in the face of this evidence you still feel that forecast long-term EPS growth rates can be reasonably accurate then you may want to use the PEG. However, things are far from simple even then. As Aswath Damodaran explains in his compendious tome *Investment Valuation,* the PEG you would expect for a fairly valued company in fact depends on the earnings growth rate, the payout ratio (what proportion of earnings are paid out as dividends) and the cost of capital. I shall not go into the details because the full PEG equation is very complicated. For several equations and a full discussion of all this, see Damodaran's book. The consequence is that dividing by the percentage growth rate does *not* mean that we can forget about growth rates from now on and blithely compare companies with different growth rates. On the contrary, it just makes the equation more complicated. Different growth rates could in fact mean that the PEG should be higher or lower.

It turns out that it is really not valid to compare the PEGs of two companies that have very different earnings growth rates, business risk or payout ratios, even if they are in the same industry. If you *can* find two such similar companies, the PEG might be valid. But then you might just as well use the P/E ratio to compare them.

# Chapter 11
## The Long-Term P/E

Why do we take into account earnings from only one year when we try to value a company using the P/E? A year is the amount of time that the Earth takes to go round the Sun, and by law the period over which companies must publish audited accounts. For many companies a year is really not relevant to their business cycle. For most companies the most important effect on their activity is the health of the economy as a whole. They should really have their earnings measured over the whole economic cycle to get a true view of their long-term earnings potential. An economic cycle is generally thought to last 7-8 years on average.

As with many good ideas, this one was first thought of decades ago, and then nothing was done with it afterwards. In *Security Analysis* in 1934, Ben Graham and David Dodd recommended the use of average earnings over a period of at least five years, and preferably over seven to ten years, as giving a much more reliable view of the true earnings potential of a company.

Something similar was suggested by Robert Shiller in his 2001 book *Irrational Exuberance*, but at the level of the overall market P/E. His ten-year 'cyclically adjusted P/E' (often abbreviated to CAPE) was, he proposed, a useful measure of how overvalued or undervalued the market as a whole was compared to its long-term average. However, no-one thought of scientifically testing Graham and Dodd's suggestion at the level of individual stocks until my paper in 2006.

I am sure this kind of thing happens all the time in many disciplines, but it brings to mind what happened to Louis Bachelier, who studied the movement of prices on the Paris Bourse. His PhD thesis in 1900 was the first to describe market prices as what we now call a 'random walk'. Unfortunately his work was far ahead of its time. Getting one's hands dirty looking at how market prices changed really did not fit into the world of academic mathematics of the time, and there was no discipline of academic finance back then. As usually happens to ideas that are right but don't fit, it was promptly forgotten about. It was eventually rediscovered by US finance researchers in the 1950s. It ultimately led, via models of how share prices move, to the Black-Scholes option pricing model in 1973 that today is used millions of times daily to price options.

Since 2008 there has been an Institut Louis Bachelier on Place de la Bourse in Paris, of which I am sure the man himself would have been very proud had he lived to see it. He would have been even prouder had someone powerful in the world of mathematics or the Bourse taken an interest in his ideas while he was still alive. Instead he spent most of the rest of his career teaching in provincial universities.

I am no Bachelier and the long-term P/E is just an incremental step along the road towards more efficient stock analysis. But *Security Analysis* is still a popular book that must have been read by millions over the decades, many of them with access to stock price databases. It does seem strange that not one of them got around to testing Graham and Dodd's suggestion about the long-term P/E until I decided to 70 years later.

## Haynes' long-term P/E

What does taking into account several back years of earnings do to a company's P/E? Let's look at Haynes again. They have an enviable record of positive earnings going back decades, but let us concentrate on the earnings over the last ten years. I use a base date of 1 May 2009 because that was the final portfolio formation date in the results reported later in this chapter and the next.

**Table 8: Haynes Publishing EPS**

| Year | 2000 | 2001 | 2002 | 2003 | 2004 | 2005 | 2006 | 2007 | 2008 | 2009 |
|------|------|------|------|------|------|------|------|------|------|------|
| EPS | 21.5 | 1.9 | 9.5 | 19.3 | 31.2 | 34.1 | 35.2 | 31.4 | 30.3 | 26.3 |

Source: DataStream

Bear in mind that this history will not agree in detail with the EPS record you get on information services such as Company REFS or from reading the annual report. DataStream's EPS figures sometimes seem to follow a logic all of their own, because they are updated when the interim results come out and are adjusted for stock splits etc.

Haynes had a share price of 148p on 1 May 2009, so the traditional historic P/E was:

$$\frac{148}{26.3} = 5.6$$

The two-year P/E was:

$$\frac{148}{\text{average } (30.3, 26.3)} = 5.2$$

And so on up to the ten-year P/E, which was:

$$\frac{148}{\text{average } (21.5, 1.9, \ldots 26.3)} = 6.1$$

So under the long-term P/E Haynes is still a value firm with a ten-year P/E of 6.1, but it no longer has quite such a low P/E because the earnings over the past five years have been unusually good. The lower earnings in the five years previous to that make the ten-year P/E higher. (In fact the average EPS we have for Haynes going back 31 years is 16.2p.) Haynes falls into ten-year P/E decile 8 in 2009. This means that at least 20% of companies had even lower P/Es than Haynes had that year, but then market-wide P/Es were particularly low then.

## What use is the long-term P/E?

To test whether these longer-term P/Es are of any use in predicting returns, I followed a fairly standard procedure that most of the papers covered in Part II also use. First I set up a database of all UK companies since 1975 (over 4000 have been quoted at some point). I then took this year by year and listed all companies that were quoted on the stock market on 30 April 1975, 30 April 1976 and so on up to 30 April 2009. This gave about 1300 companies available to invest in in each year group, although the companies themselves change (the average company is only quoted for seven years before it is taken over or disappears for some other reason).

Then, for each year, I sorted them by their traditional (one year) P/Es and divided them into ten groups (deciles), so as to mirror having bought ten portfolios: the lowest 10% of companies by P/E, the next 10% and so on up to the highest 10% of companies by P/E. Then I calculated the average returns including dividends for each of those ten groups assuming I had held all the stocks for one year, i.e. 1 May

1975 - 30 April 1976, 1 May 1976 - 30 April 1977, and so un until 1 May 2009 - 30 April 2010.

The difference to previous papers is that I was adjusting the sort statistic as I went along. So at first I sorted all the companies by the traditional P/E and calculated the average returns for all the one-year holding periods from 1975-6 up to 2009-10. Then I did it all over again but sorted them by the two-year P/E. It was all the same companies and the same one-year returns for each, but some of them fell into a different portfolio group due to their P/E changing, as we just saw for Haynes. And so on, up to sorting by the ten-year P/E.

Adding more years of earnings to the earnings part of the P/E does greatly increase the power of the P/E to predict returns, as Table 9 shows.

**Table 9: Average one-year returns for decile portfolios of all UK stocks 1975-2009. Companies are sorted into portfolios each year using the traditional P/E ratio (PE1) through to PE10 (the current share price divided by the average annual EPS over the last ten years)**

| | PE1 | PE2 | PE3 | PE4 | PE5 | PE6 | PE7 | PE8 | PE9 | PE10 |
|---|---|---|---|---|---|---|---|---|---|---|
| High P/E | 14.23% | 14.55% | 15.50% | 15.46% | 15.11% | 15.40% | 15.27% | 14.46% | 13.27% | 12.18% |
| Decile 2 | 15.27% | 16.56% | 14.23% | 15.01% | 15.42% | 15.40% | 14.90% | 15.30% | 14.67% | 14.27% |
| Decile 3 | 16.35% | 16.63% | 17.24% | 17.69% | 16.79% | 15.96% | 15.17% | 14.05% | 14.08% | 15.16% |
| Decile 4 | 15.22% | 16.64% | 16.42% | 16.15% | 16.78% | 14.89% | 15.19% | 15.70% | 15.39% | 13.07% |
| Decile 5 | 14.87% | 14.58% | 14.75% | 14.82% | 14.46% | 16.67% | 15.92% | 15.39% | 15.52% | 15.99% |
| Decile 6 | 16.09% | 16.68% | 17.05% | 15.61% | 15.46% | 15.58% | 16.85% | 16.90% | 16.71% | 16.51% |
| Decile 7 | 17.65% | 15.73% | 16.35% | 17.27% | 17.95% | 16.47% | 15.67% | 15.91% | 16.00% | 14.77% |
| Decile 8 | 16.97% | 17.34% | 17.53% | 18.39% | 17.53% | 17.67% | 16.32% | 15.58% | 16.08% | 16.54% |
| Decile 9 | 19.59% | 16.53% | 16.35% | 16.40% | 17.68% | 18.04% | 18.57% | 18.03% | 17.47% | 16.46% |
| Low P/E | 19.91% | 19.11% | 18.30% | 18.61% | 19.41% | 19.30% | 20.56% | 21.42% | 21.16% | 21.63% |
| D10–D1 | 5.67% | 4.56% | 2.79% | 3.15% | 4.30% | 3.90% | 5.29% | 6.96% | 7.89% | 9.45% |

The top left-hand cell in Table 9 means that, if you had taken the highest 10% of companies sorting by one-year historical P/E, each year from 30 April 1975 to 30 April 2009, and held them as a portfolio for one year, you would have got average returns of 14.23% per year. This sounds a very good return, but not if you compare it to what you would have got doing the same thing but with the *lowest* 10% of companies sorted by the one-year historical P/E. Doing that, you would have averaged 19.91% a year ('Low P/E', leftmost cell). The difference between those two average returns is the final 'D10 - D1' row: 5.67% a year.

As we move across the table from left to right, it shows the average returns from decile portfolios created after sorting by the traditional P/E, then by the two-year P/E, and so on across to the right-most column which shows the returns when sorting companies into P/E portfolios using the ten-year P/E. Don't worry about the returns shown in the 'decile 2' to 'decile 9' rows. Those are mainly there to show that the returns do go up fairly smoothly as you move through the deciles, so the D10-D1 row isn't just some random figure. What we are really interested in is the difference in average returns between the high P/E and low P/E decile portfolios: D10-D1 in the final row. This is the P/E 'value premium' and the measure of how useful our statistic is at predicting returns. It's shown in the final row.

The D10-D1 value premium for the traditional P/E (PE1) of 5.67% is much as we would expect: in most published tests, the lowest 10% of stocks by P/E outperforms the highest 10% of stocks by 5-6% a year on average. This difference drops off initially as we go from left to right in the final row including more and more past years of earnings into the P/E calculation. It starts to rise again when we are including five or more years of past earnings. This may be why the long-term P/E has not become popular before, if anyone has tried this but used shorter earnings histories – they were simply not including enough years of earnings to improve on the traditional P/E. In the rightmost column, calculating the P/E using the average of the last ten years of earnings increases the power of the P/E to predict returns by two-thirds (9.45% versus 5.67%).

Averaging the historic earnings assumes that each past year has an equally useful amount of information about the company's long-term earnings power. Since economic conditions and company profiles change over time, last year's earnings should be a much better guide than earnings from ten years ago, shouldn't they?

Apparently not.

No matter how I arranged the weights, I couldn't get anything to work significantly better than a simple average. What's more, *P/Es calculated using the individual one-year earnings from six or more years ago worked better than the traditional P/E.* Clearly, the true earnings potential of a firm is a very long-lived phenomenon. The P/E obviously doesn't change through time as most people think. If anyone is reading this book in 50 years' time, that is what I suggest they look at.

## Running high and low P/E portfolios

We can run a historical back-test to show how we would have fared had we been running high and low P/E-based portfolios since 1975. Figure 7 shows the great increase in power for the P/E that we could have harnessed by taking into account earnings from previous years.

**Figure 7: Portfolio values for the value and glamour deciles using PE1 and PE10 to sort companies into deciles. PE10 is the P/E calculated using average earnings over the last ten years.**

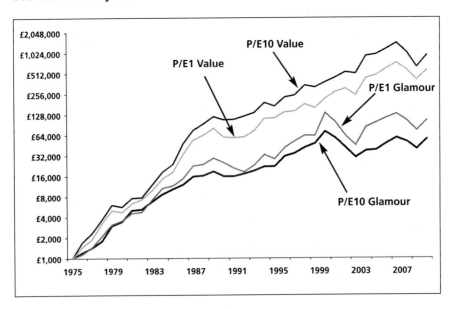

The chart shows how you would have done if you had bought the highest and lowest 10% of stocks by P/E each year, held them for one year, sold them, recalculated your P/Es and bought the next lot. We are mirroring running P/E-based value and glamour portfolios. First of all we use the traditional P/E to decide what is a value stock and what is a glamour stock. This gives the two middle lines.

The two lines outside them are doing exactly the same thing, but assume you had used the ten-year P/E every year since 1975 to sort your stocks into portfolios, instead of the traditional one-year P/E. All four portfolios start off with £1000 each in 1975.

The difference in performance might not look huge, but that is because of the logarithmic scale. Using the ten-year long-term P/E, the value portfolio ends up in May 2010 being worth 65% more than it would have been using the traditional P/E (£948,000 compared to £575,000). On the other side of the value-glamour split, taking more years into account means that the long-term P/E is better at identifying poorly performing glamour shares too (useful if you are running a long-short portfolio for a hedge fund). The difference for the glamour portfolio is more marked: the PE10 glamour portfolio ends up worth only £56,000 in May 2010, compared to £105,000 for glamour firms according to the traditional P/E.

Even £56,000 might seem like very respectable returns, but that is a compound return over 35 years of 12.18% per annum. These figures are not inflation-adjusted, and remember that inflation touched 26% in the 1970s. Gilts would have yielded you around 8% p.a. and that is giving a guaranteed positive return every year. Share portfolios fall in a significant minority of years, so beating gilts by just 4% given the extra risk you would have taken is nothing to be proud of.

Using publicly available information and a not-particularly-clever method, just sorting shares into portfolios in a different way, taking into account their earnings from previous years, we have boosted our value portfolio returns quite significantly by using long-term information in the P/E. Alternatively, we can predictably get even worse returns in the case of glamour shares.

This alone seems to beg the question: how efficient is the stock market really? I was working alone on my PC with some Excel data from DataStream. Surely a team of bank analysts using Matlab could do far better?

There are further ways in which the P/E can be improved, and we look at these in the next two chapters.

# Chapter 12
**Decomposing the P/E**

As we have seen previously, there are many influences on the P/E that cannot be ascribed to the company itself. Four in particular should be clear to any experienced investor and are explained below. I do not claim that this is an exhaustive list. Indeed there are almost certainly other influences on the P/E that I have not allowed for. However, these are the factors that are considered in the work that follows.

Could allowing for how these influences affect the P/E make it a more useful statistic? This is what I try to answer in this and the following chapter.

Note that, building on the previous chapter, all the P/Es referred to from now on are the ten-year P/E, i.e. the P/E calculated using the average of the past ten years of earnings as the denominator.

I suggest four influences on a company's P/E:

1.  The **year**: the average market P/E varies year by year, as the overall level of investor confidence changes.

2.  The **sector** in which the company operates. Average earnings in the computer services sector, for example, are growing faster (at least averaged over decades, notwithstanding blips such as the 2000-3 dot-com crash) than in the water supply sector. Companies in sectors that are growing faster in the long-term deserve to get a higher P/E. They can expect a faster-growing future stream of earnings, so you should expect to pay more now for each £1 of future years' earnings.

3.  The **size** of the company. For people in finance (academics or market players) this is invariably measured by the market capitalisation. Accountants usually use the book value of assets, since it is one of their statistics and the share price moves around so much. Some researchers have used the number of employees. This could be useful if you are looking at a service company with few tangible assets where most of its potential is inside the heads of its employees. However you measure it, large companies tend to have considerably higher P/Es than small ones, and this is quite a close straight-line relationship.

4.  **Idiosyncratic effects.** Companies examined in the same year, operating in the same sector and of similar sizes nevertheless have different P/Es. I use the term 'idiosyncratic effects' to talk about these. These could be anything from the announcement of a large contract, whether the directors have recently bought

or sold shares, to how warmly the company is recommended by analysts. Most of these factors won't affect any other company.

How can we allow for how these influences affect the P/E?

A parallel that some readers may have come across before is DuPont analysis. Return on Assets (ROA) is defined as net income divided by total assets, so it is a measure of how hard company management are making the assets work to produce income. However, ROA can be *decomposed* as follows:

$$\text{ROA} = \frac{\text{net income}}{\text{total assets}} = \frac{\text{net income}}{\text{sales}} \times \frac{\text{sales}}{\text{total assets}}$$

The first fraction in the right-hand side of the equation, net income divided by sales, tells you the company's profit margin. The second fraction, sales/total assets, tells you the rate of asset turnover: how efficiently the company is using its assets to generate sales revenue. Thus a simple decomposition can tell you much more than the simple ROA about how efficiently the company is operating.

With the decomposed P/E I am trying to do something similar, though not exactly parallel, on each company's P/E. What I did was extract each of the four influences given above from a company's P/E:

$$\frac{\text{actual EP}}{\text{average EP}} = \frac{\text{year EP}}{\text{average EP}} \times \frac{\text{size EP}}{\text{average EP}} \times \frac{\text{sector EP}}{\text{average EP}} \times \frac{\text{idiosynchratic EP}}{\text{average EP}}$$

This is clearly different to the ROA decomposition. I am saying that the observed P/E is a product of four factors. The first three are independently observable: the average P/E for that year, for that size category of company, and for that sector. The final factor, the idiosyncratic P/E, is not independently observable, but is the P/E that will make the equation balance.

Since I am dividing each P/E on the right-hand side by the average P/E across the whole dataset, each factor will have a value of one for a completely average company. If a company is part of a sector that has a very high P/E, for example, but its actual

P/E is average across all companies, then it will have to have a particularly low idiosyncratic P/E to compensate.

I then calculated each factor's power to predict returns, weighted them accordingly, and put them back together again. The 'decomposed P/E' may thus be a misnomer, in that it is a decomposed, non-company-specific factors weighted and then put-back-together-again P/E, but 'decomposed P/E' has stuck for want of a better name.

The most important finding was that the sector effect works the opposite way round to the others, so it gets reversed before the P/E is reassembled, which is what the reverse arrow is meant to show in Figure 8. You end up with a much more powerful P/E because it no longer has different factors pulling in different directions.

**Figure 8: Decomposing the influences on the P/E ratio**

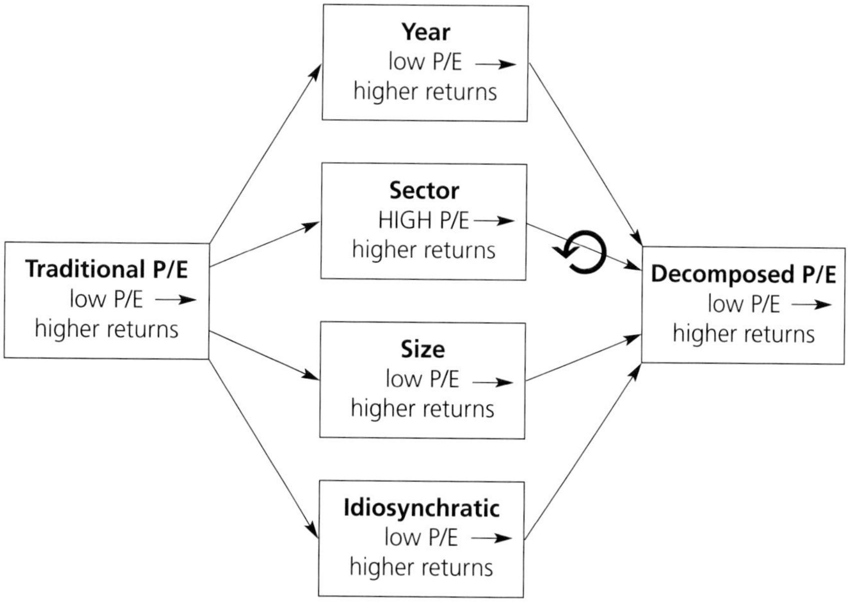

Let's take a more detailed look at each of these factors in turn.

# The year effect

How much the market-wide P/E varies through time can be seen in Figure 9.

**Figure 9: Market-wide average ten-year P/Es, 1975-2009**

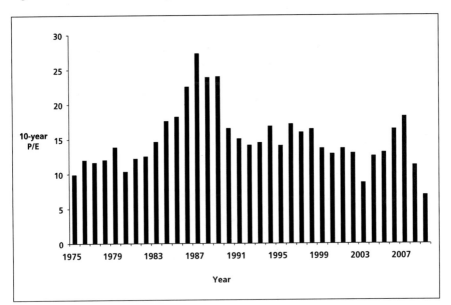

The market-wide P/E varies by a factor of three over the years, from a peak of 27.3 before the Black Wednesday crash of October 1987 down to a historic low of 6.9 in 2009. The higher the market-wide P/E is in any year, the lower the market returns tend to be next year. People have suggested using the market-wide P/E as a buy/sell signal – this is called 'market timing'. Sadly it seems that the market-wide P/E is rather an unreliable predictor of average returns. Stocks outperform gilts by several percentage points a year on average, and the market-wide P/E just isn't reliable enough an indicator to make up this gap. It is still better to stay invested in stocks at all times.

The market-wide P/E for that year is the most powerful influence on every individual company's P/E, as we shall see below.

# The sector effect

Companies can be split up into many different sectors. The average P/Es of these sectors vary widely here too, from 7.8 to 42.5. The significant result here is that a lower sector P/E means *poorer* returns. This is the only place you will ever see this: wherever and whenever the P/E is tested, a lower P/E points to better returns. Of the hundreds of academic research papers written on the P/E, none claim that higher P/Es lead to higher returns, at least outside the run-up to the tech stock boom in 1999-2000. However in this sole instance the opposite is true. The software sector with its high average P/E of 20.7 really does give better returns on average than the auto parts sector (P/E 8.3), presumably because software as a whole is growing more quickly in the long-term, regardless of the returns on individual companies.

The sector P/E effect within the overall P/E has *an opposite effect* on overall returns compared to that of the other effects. The decomposed P/E allows for this fact. Using it, unloved companies from growth sectors have a greater chance of being chosen as value shares than they do with the normal P/E. Traditional value funds are inevitably made up of a mixture of stocks from value sectors and value stocks from glamour sectors, but the latter are likely to produce higher returns.

One question you might ask here is whether this will persist in future. If I redid the research in 20 years time, would the ranking of sectors still be the same? My feeling is that the overall view will be the same, but the details will be different. Steel will still be low growth, because it has been for decades, but nanotechnology and industries that don't exist yet will be high growth. The sectors with high P/Es will still be giving slightly better returns.

## The size effect

Large companies usually command a higher P/E than small companies. Simple logistical problems faced by fund managers trying to trade millions of shares at a time are probably most of the reason for this. The fund manager really is dependent on the deep liquidity large company shares offer. Otherwise as soon as he tries to buy or sell large blocks of shares, or a large private client manager issues buy or sell advice to its clients, he is going to move the market against himself.[6] Managers of large funds therefore naturally gravitate towards investing in larger companies. Since they run most of the money in the market, they pay a price for this.

---

[6] On a visit to a company with tens of thousands of private clients, I was told that their analysts cover only FTSE 100 and (rarely) FTSE-250 stocks. Imagine the chaos that would ensue if 400 private client managers tried to advise their hundred clients each to buy or sell the same thinly traded AIM stock on the same day.

I divided companies into 20 size categories (calculated within each year as the average market capitalisation has grown so much over the years) and worked out the average P/E and returns for each size category. See Figure 10.

**Figure 10: Average 10-year P/E by market size category, 1975-2009**

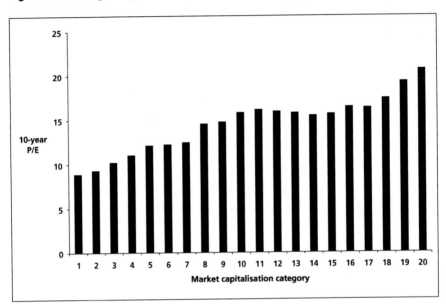

There is a close relationship, albeit not quite a straight-line relationship, between the size category and the P/E. Unsurprisingly, given the connection between P/Es and returns, average annual returns varied in a fairly straight line too, but going down from left to right. They ranged from 26.1% per annum for the smallest 5% of companies to 17% for the largest.

As with using the market-wide P/E for a market timing rule, however, there are problems if you thought to use only this as a trading rule, investing in the smallest stocks and forgetting about the P/E. Not only does the size premium come and go over the years, as Professors Dimson and Marsh at London Business School discovered. That is already included in the 26.1% versus 17.0%. The excellent returns of the smallest stocks could also be very much eroded depending on how often you trade. For the smallest companies, each time you bought then sold you would incur an average 8.2% charge on the bid-ask spread, compared to only 1% for the largest stocks.

# Constructing the decomposed P/E

Having shown how these individual factors work within the P/E, we are now ready to construct the decomposed P/E. After pulling each of the factors out, I gave them weights according to how useful each factor was in predicting returns. Then I put them back together to form the decomposed P/E. As you can see looking back at Figure 8, the really important point here was that not only did these factors have different values, *one of them was working against the others*, wrapped up inside the P/E as it is currently used. Take out the sector factor, spin it around by reversing its sign and put it back in, and suddenly you have a P/E that is much more useful. This is despite the fact that we are using only information that is publicly available. Again, it doesn't make the market look very efficient.

I shall not go through the details of the linear regression and weighting system here. Suffice it to say that I used a linear regression[7] to decide which components of the P/E give us the most useful information about returns in the future. I separated out the components and weighted them[8] according to their usefulness, then put them back together to arrive at the decomposed P/E. So it's really a decomposed, weighted and put-back-together-again P/E.

It turns out that the year P/E is roughly twice as useful in predicting returns as the size P/E, which in turn is twice as useful a predictor as the sector and idiosyncratic P/Es. The sector P/E works the opposite way round to the others, as I explained above, so its weight is the only one to have a negative sign in the equation for the decomposed P/E.

---

[7] Linear regression: I take these factors just described and set them up as an equation:

Rtn = a + b*YearPE + c*industryPE + d*sizePE + error term

for each of the thousands of one-year company returns observed over the years 1975-2009. The computer does the regression and gives the values for a, b, c, and d that most closely 'predict' the returns we have actually observed.

[8] Weighting: the signs and relative sizes of the values for a–d that the computer arrived at.

## Haynes and the decomposed P/E

Let's try to make this clearer using the example of Haynes again. Recall that in 2009 they had a price of 148p, a ten-year P/E of 6.1 and fell into long-term P/E decile 8. How do all these adjustments affect their P/E?

**Year P/E:** the average P/E for every company across every year is 13.8. The average P/E for all companies in 2009 was 6.9, the lowest it has been since at least 1975.

**Sector P/E:** Haynes' sector (Publishing) has an average P/E of 14.4, so slightly on the high side.

**Size P/E:** Haynes' market capitalisation according to DataStream was £10.88m, so in 2009 they fell into market value category 2 – not the smallest 5% of firms but the next one up. Companies falling into market value category 2 have an average P/E of 9.3, so considerably less than the average for all companies over all years because they are so small.

**Idiosyncratic P/E:** Putting all these into the decomposed P/E equation, we eventually get that the part of Haynes' overall P/E that remains unexplained by the market-wide, size and sector P/Es is 17.4. I include the following for those who want a complete explanation, but feel free to skip over it if you do not:

(Note that we are using ten-year E/Ps so we have to divide by 10 and then take the inverse to get a meaningful P/E.)

$$\text{average EP} = 0.7239; \quad \frac{10}{0.7239} = 13.8141$$

$$\text{year EP} = 1.4419; \quad \frac{10}{1.4419} = 6.9353$$

$$\text{size EP} = 1.0751; \quad \frac{10}{1.0751} = 9.3015$$

$$\text{sector EP} = 0.6929; \quad \frac{10}{0.7238} = 14.4342$$

$$\text{actual EP} = 1.6262; \quad \frac{10}{1.6261} = 6.1497$$

Rearranging the decomposed P/E equation:

$$\text{idio EP} = \frac{\text{actual EP} \times \text{average EP}^3}{\text{year EP} \times \text{size EP} \times \text{sector EP}} = \frac{1.6262 \times 0.7239^3}{1.4419 \times 1.0751 \times 0.6929} = 0.5744$$

$$\text{one-year P/E} = \frac{10}{0.5744} = 17.41$$

Having worked out the idiosyncratic P/E, we can now weight these decomposed parts of the P/E and put them back together. Again, skip over this if you do not want all the details of the calculation. Each line shows the regression coefficient times the EP:

year EP: 0.3569 x 1.4419 = 0.5146

size EP: 0.1587 x 1.0751 = 0.1706

sector EP: -0.0795 x 0.6929 = -0.05551

idio EP: 0.0742 x 0.5744 = 0.0426

sum = 0.6727

The sum of the coefficients is 0.5103, so we must divide by this to get a ten-year EP:

$$\frac{0.6727}{0.5103} = 1.3182$$

decomposed PE $\frac{10}{1.3182} = 7.6$

which is in decile 9 of all decomposed PEs in 2009

So weighting the four components and reassembling them means that Haynes' decomposed P/E of 7.6 falls into decile 9 compared to all the other companies' decomposed P/Es. The company has therefore moved up one from the decile 8 that it occupied according to its ten-year P/E. They are a very small firm and that makes them move upwards. Also their sector P/E is high, and that makes them move up too – recall that the sector P/E works in the opposite way to the other P/E influences. The idiosyncratic P/E is on the high side so that moves them down again, but the overall effect is to move them up one decile.

## Testing the decomposed P/E

And how well does sorting by the new decomposed P/E work overall? This can be seen in Table 10. We have widened further the difference between the top and bottom 10% of stocks when sorting them by the decomposed P/E, to 11.34%. It is hard to see how this large difference could be explained away when we have only used information that was already available for free.

**Table 10: Annual returns by portfolio decile for the traditional P/E, the ten-year P/E and the decomposed P/E, 1975-2009. (The returns shown for the traditional P/E are different to those in Table 9 because we are using only companies with a full ten years of positive earnings here.)**

|  | P/E1 | P/E10 | Decomposed P/E |
|---|---|---|---|
| High P/E | 14.06% | 12.18% | 10.65% |
| Decile 2 | 15.11% | 14.27% | 11.30% |
| Decile 3 | 14.62% | 15.16% | 12.95% |
| Decile 4 | 12.45% | 13.07% | 15.68% |
| Decile 5 | 16.60% | 16.01% | 13.86% |
| Decile 6 | 14.73% | 16.51% | 16.28% |
| Decile 7 | 16.46% | 14.81% | 18.06% |
| Decile 8 | 16.36% | 16.51% | 18.24% |
| Decile 9 | 16.37% | 16.46% | 18.49% |
| Low P/E | 19.90% | 21.64% | 21.99% |
| D10 – D1 | 5.84% | 9.46% | 11.34% |

Another portfolio illustration should show the widening power of the P/E that we now have at our fingertips. Figure 8 compares the returns for the decomposed P/E value and glamour portfolios to those for the ten-year P/E, in which the influences of year average P/E, size P/E and industry P/E had not yet been differentiated. The traditional P/E is also there for comparison.

**Figure 11: Performances of glamour and value deciles for the traditional P/E, the ten-year P/E and the decomposed P/E**

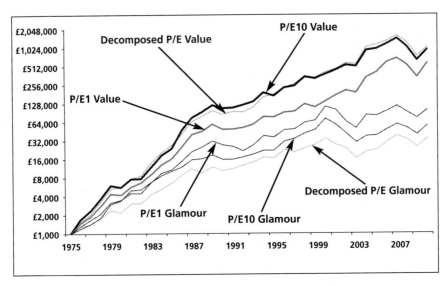

The Y-axis uses a logarithmic scale. For the value portfolios, the decomposed P/E portfolio ends up being worth 10% more than the ten-year P/E-based portfolio (£1,049,000 versus £951,000). The big improvement here is in distinguishing poorly performing glamour portfolios: the decomposed P/E glamour portfolio ends up worth 42% less than the PE10-based portfolio (£35,000 versus £56,000). The decomposed P/E glamour decile has in fact only returned 10.65% p.a. This is barely more than gilts would have returned over those years, but with a lot more risk. Whether the market is functioning efficiently here seems seriously in doubt.

# Chapter 13
## A Cautionary Tale: The Naked P/E

The Naked P/E is the same thing as the 'idiosyncratic P/E' used in the previous chapter. Every company has a different P/E, even compared to another company at the same time, operating in the same sector and having the same market capitalisation. Thus the 'Naked P/E' is that part of the P/E that can't be attributed to the year in which the company's P/E was measured, the sector it was operating in or its size, as I explained at the start of the previous chapter. At first I named this part of the P/E the Idiosyncratic P/E, and it is called that in Chapter 12. At the suggestion of a colleague with a better nose for promoting a new idea than I have, it soon became the much snappier Naked P/E.

It turns out that the Naked P/E is particularly useful for identifying extreme value and glamour stocks, and making up portfolios of a few shares that have extraordinarily good performances (or extraordinarily bad ones, if you use it to identify glamour shares). There is a 16.4% annual gap in returns between these extreme value and glamour portfolios, which I demonstrate in the final portfolio example.

The usual thing you see in academic papers (and what I did in Chapters 11 and 12) involves dividing stocks into deciles and seeing which statistics are the best at predicting returns. What you very rarely see, presumably because academic finance researchers don't run their own portfolios, is someone taking the top and bottom *n* stocks, where *n* is some small number from 1 to 50, and see which statistics work best choosing *those* portfolios. Those portfolios are the type that real investors usually hold. Show me a private investor with 200 stocks in his portfolio, as the Fidelity Special Situations fund has, and I'll show you someone who's rich enough to employ a portfolio manager full time (or a poor man who has been crucified by trading costs).

I began the same as in the previous two chapters, but fixed the size of the portfolio at ten shares. I then proceeded as in the previous chapter, testing which of the components of the P/E were most useful for choosing these sort of extreme value or glamour stocks. It soon became clear that the Naked P/E was by far the most useful statistic to sort by if it is supposed to pick up the extreme ends of the spectrum. The sector and size factors had little extra information to give here. Although sector and size exert a big influence on company returns in general, they weren't much use in spotting the companies with the highest returns of all. Since these companies are the most mispriced in the market, it seems reasonable to suppose there are unique things about them that deter investors.

Since we are talking about extreme shares here, let's take an extreme example. On 30 April 2009 shares in Johnston Press were trading at 15.5p, but the average of their previous ten years of earnings was 21.1p EPS per year. Thus they had a ten-year P/E of 0.7. The P/E for the market as a whole then was very low historically at 6.9. They were worth £99m and such mid-sized companies merited a size P/E of 12.5. The sector (Publishing) had a slightly high P/E of 14.4. Putting all these together in the equation given in the previous chapter, this gave them a Naked P/E of 1.5: twice the simple ten-year P/E, but still the most attractive Naked P/E on the whole market on that day. Johnston Press shares went up by 115% in the next year. This of course is exceptional, but not that exceptional: the ten most attractive stocks on that day went up by an average 55% over the next year.

## How many shares should you hold?

I therefore proceeded using the Naked P/E, i.e. that part of a company's P/E that cannot be attributed to the market average P/E, nor to the company's size and sector P/Es. I ignored these other influences, since they seemed to have little to tell me about the future returns of these extremely overvalued or undervalued stocks. We now take that as fixed and vary the number of shares in the portfolio instead.

*What is the best number of shares to hold to get the best returns?*

The answer can be seen in Figures 12 and 13. These figures are for arithmetic mean returns rather than the geometric mean returns that we have used up to now, for reasons that will become clear.

**Figure 12: Annual returns for value, glamour and arbitrage small portfolios of 5-50 shares, 1975-2009**

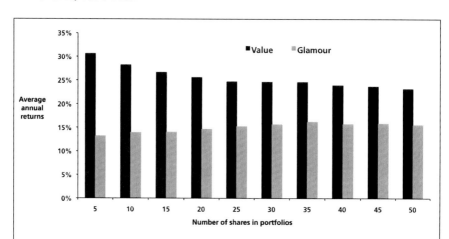

The fewer, the better, it appears, with a five-share value portfolio giving just over 30% a year. Let's zoom in to have a look at the chart for 1-15 shares:

**Figure 13: Average annual returns for *very* small portfolios of 1-15 shares, 1975-2009**

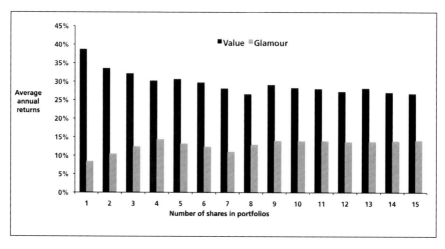

So if you were brave enough each year to hold the one share on the market with the lowest Naked P/E, the average annual returns were 38.6%. However, the fewer shares you have, the more risky your portfolio becomes. In this extreme case, your one share might give excellent returns most years, but if there is one year when that company goes bankrupt then you are out of the game for good. What is the best portfolio size, taking this extra riskiness into account?

## Allowing for risk

You can compare a portfolio's returns to its riskiness using the Sharpe Ratio.[9] This is what is commonly used to compare the performance of fund managers. A fund manager who loads up on high beta stocks, and then outperforms their competitors because of a general market rise, hasn't really outperformed them. He or she has just been lucky to have been holding high-beta stocks when the market rose. The Sharpe ratio takes account of this portfolio risk and allows a fair ranking.

**Figure 14: Sharpe Ratios of very small value, glamour and arbitrage portfolios of *n* shares, 1975-2009**

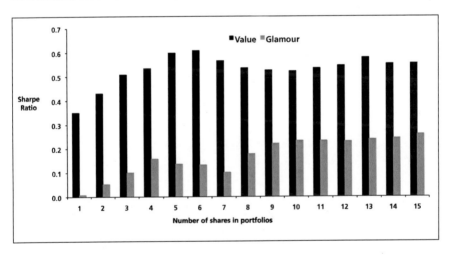

---

[9] The Sharpe Ratio is $S = \frac{R - R_f}{\sigma}$ , i.e. the arithmetic mean portfolio returns over and above the risk-free rate, stated as a proportion of the standard deviation of returns. It is the most popular indicator of a portfolio's riskiness, although it relies on the same problematic idea as the CAPM that risk can be measured by volatility.

The Sharpe Ratio of the one-share portfolio is much smaller, because that 38.6% return was won at the cost of extreme riskiness. In fact the one-share portfolio has a variability of returns (standard deviation) of more than twice that of a portfolio with only four shares. Another way to look at this is the difference between arithmetic and geometric mean returns. If returns are the same every year, these two are the same. But the more returns vary, the more geometric returns suffer compared to average returns. In the extreme case, if you have just one year of returns of -100%, i.e. a total loss, your geometric returns for the whole period will be -100% as well: you were wiped out. In the case of the one-share portfiolio, although the *arithmetic* mean annual returns were 38.6%, the *geometric* mean (the 35th root of what you would have been left with in May 2010 from actually holding one share per year as your portfolio) was only 11.4% per year. And it is the geometric mean that is the important figure if you are worried about what you are left with at the end of the day.

## A final portfolio example

We can now demonstrate the wide gap in returns we have opened up between the value and glamour stocks. The example also vividly illustrates the riskiness of holding a few stocks in turbulent economic times. It uses the five share value portfolio as an example and compares it to its matching glamour portfolio.

**Figure 15: £1000 invested in the five lowest Naked P/E value shares, the five highest Naked P/E glamour shares, and an equally weighted market average, rebalanced annually, 1975-2009**

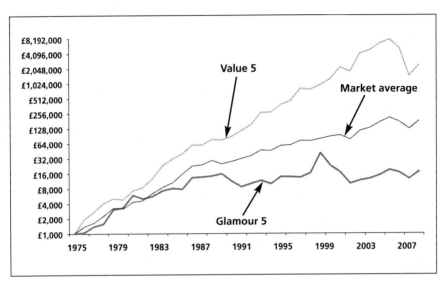

The value portfolio turns £1000 in 1975 into £2,393,000 in 2010, at an annual compound rate of 24.9%. However, it *was* worth £7,782,000 in 2007, which was a compound return of 32.3% over the 32 years from 1975 to 2007, so it has dropped off quite alarmingly since.

Since the performance of the five-share value portfolio was so bad in 2008-9 but very good in 2009-10, and there are only five shares in each portfolio each year, compared to the dozens of stocks we had when we were looking at decile portfolios for the long-term P/E and decomposed P/E, let's take a look at the individual companies the computer selected and their returns:

**Tables 11a and 11b: Individual companies and one-year returns for the Naked P/E 5-share value portfolios, 2008-9 and 2009-10**

| Company | Return 2008-9 |
| --- | --- |
| Taylor Woodrow plc | -61% |
| Barratt Developments | -48% |
| Regent Inns plc | -93% |
| SMG plc | -68% |
| Wagon plc | -92% |
| Average | -72% |

| Company | Return 2009-10 |
| --- | --- |
| Barratt Developments | +35% |
| Dawson Holdings plc | -57% |
| Trinity Mirror plc | +167% |
| SMG plc | +65% |
| Johnston Press plc | +115% |
| Average | +65% |

In 2008-9 the portfolio lost almost three-quarters of its value, with every share losing money. The best performance was from Barratt which lost 48%. Clearly the Naked P/E might tell us which shares are incorrectly valued, but it doesn't necessarily tell us when is a good time to buy them.

In fact the market went down and down to finally reach its bottom in February 2009. At this point there were some remarkable bargains available, if you had the bottle to ignore the apparently imminent collapse of the Western financial system.

This wasn't known in May 2008 though. If I had bought those shares as a fund manager in May 2008 then I would have been out of a job shortly thereafter. This is why this chapter is entitled 'a cautionary tale'. The Naked P/E might be powerful but it clearly needs to be combined with other indicators if you want to keep your sanity and your wealth intact.

Nevertheless, some of the damage was repaired in the following year. Only Dawson Holdings fell in value and two of the shares more than doubled. A 72% loss followed by a 65% gain by no means got us back to where we started from. Instead it left us with a portfolio worth 46% of what it had been two years earlier. (0.28 x 1.65 = 0.46).

The glamour portfolio in the chart ends up worth £17,411, i.e. a compound return of 8.5%, more or less what we could have made from holding gilts over the 35 years, so it would have a Sharpe Ratio close to zero. It also incurred a much higher risk, running up losses in 12 years. So this even more clearly suggests that the market is overvaluing the returns it expects from these shares, contrary to the efficient markets hypothesis.

# Chapter 14

**Have We Rescued the P/E?**

Part III started at the point where the P/E had largely fallen by the wayside, at least in academic finance circles if not in the investment management industry. Fama and French chose not to use it as their value indicator in their three-factor model, although I argued that they didn't test it on a level playing field with price-to-book value. Even Lakonishok, Schleifer and Vishny said it was flawed, because true value stocks that have had one bad year get a high P/E and so appear in the glamour portfolio.

We have looked at some of the limited work that has been done to improve how the P/E works. In fact very little has been done. There must be a lot of scope for adjusting the earnings calculation, for example, so it only includes those items that are most relevant to a firm's long-term earnings potential. Tony Kang made a start by only including operating earnings, but people could easily try excluding other things, or weighting some sorts of earnings more heavily than others. This would be designed solely to give us an optimal predictor of future returns and it would be meaningless to accountants. One such system is covered in Joel Greenblatt's 'Magic Formula' in Chapter 16.

In the last three chapters I have shown various ways from my own research in which the P/E could be rehabilitated. From a difference between the top and bottom 10% of P/E stocks of 5.67%, using the average of the past ten past years of earnings to get a longer-term view increased this gap to 9.45%. Taking a long-term view of past earnings should solve LSV's objection to the P/E, that value firms that had had one bad year were wrongly being included amongst glamour stocks.

Unpacking the P/E into its constituent parts and repackaging them so as to maximise the P/E's usefulness to investors, we got the difference up to 11.34%. The important point from this is that the sector P/E effect has until now been working against the other effects that are wrapped up inside the traditional P/E. I extracted it, reversed its effect and put it back in, thus increasing the P/E's power. And finally, if you use the Naked P/E and very small portfolios, you get a quite extraordinary gap between the value and glamour returns of 16.4%, despite the sharp fall the value portfolio saw in 2007-9.

The example at the end shows the power of the Naked P/E when you apply it to extreme value shares: £1000 in 1975 is turned into £2.4m in 2010, at a compound rate of 24.9%. For the glamour share portfolio, £1000 is turned into £17,411, at a compound rate of 8.5%. This return is similar to what you could have got from holding gilts, but at a considerably greater risk.

All these portfolios are constructed using a handful of data series that are all publicly available. That I could do this working alone on a simple PC seems to be a considerable challenge to efficient markets. The results should also amply demonstrate that the P/E has life in it yet.

Our knowledge of the decomposed P/E and the practical experience with the Naked P/E demonstrates there is more to value than earnings. A network of factors influences the future earnings and therefore the present value of a company. Whether we employ them in a single sophisticated statistic, or use a battery of statistics, we need to consider them. In Part IV I consider candidates for statistics that could be used alongside the P/E.

# PART IV
## Beyond the P/E

In Part II I looked at the mass of work showing that low P/E stocks on average outperform the market by roughly 3% a year, and glamour stocks underperform it. To be honest, this is quite a limited result. If you were trying to follow a value share investment strategy by buying low P/E stocks, but bought and sold small stocks and incurred a lot of trading costs (the bid-ask spread is much wider for small stocks) you could easily lose the advantage that low P/E stocks offer over an index tracker, and have done a lot more work to boot. Similarly, unless you diversify across many stocks, one or two of your holdings going bust could also wipe out that 3% gain, but diversifying across many stocks also has its costs in terms of trading costs and your own time.

Part III came to the rescue, introducing several developments that promise a more powerful P/E. However, we saw in Chapter 13 that you can go too far with your cleverness if you use just one indicator without taking account of other factors.

This is what Part IV is about. Financial analysis and stock-picking is about a lot more than using just one indicator. A book of this size cannot hope to do justice to the complex subjects of financial analysis and the infinite number of different stock filters you might care to use. Instead, I look at the work of three men who have shown how the P/E can be a valuable part of a more complex stock-screening program.

Ben Graham should need no introduction. The father of value investing evolved several stock screens throughout his life to identify companies that boasted a generous helping of his 'margin of safety'. All had the P/E as a central component.

Successful US hedge fund manager Joel Greenblatt has recently written the short and very popular *Little Book that Beats the Market*. His filter is much simpler, but like Graham he wants to find value stocks that aren't going to go bust. His value indicator is the earnings yield (the reciprocal of the P/E) although he has developed his own special version of it.

Finally we take a detailed look at the work of Joseph Piotroski. He isn't yet as well known as the other two and isn't a fund manager either, but an accounting professor at Stanford. His 2000 paper introduced a simple way to summarise how financially stable a company is. Using low price-to-book value shares, he showed that the most financially stable companies outperform the least stable by a very wide margin – so wide that it brings market efficiency much more into question than my new flavours of the P/E in Part III did. It seems that analysts are nowhere near properly including the financial stability of a firm as a factor in its share price, at least for smaller companies.

Since no-one has yet tried this outside the US, I re-tested Piotroski's work specially for this book, using both PTBV and the P/E, with surprising results.

# Chapter 15

## Ben Graham: The P/E and the Margin of Safety

Despite assumptions to the contrary, Ben Graham did believe that markets are efficient. Eventually. He also believed that at any one time there are plenty of mispriced stocks out there for anyone who cared to look:

> I can assure the reader that among the 500-odd NYSE issues selling below seven times earnings today, there are plenty to be found for which the prices are not 'correct' ones, in any meaningful sense of the term. They are clearly worth more than current selling prices, and any security analyst worth his salt should be able to make up an attractive portfolio out of this 'universe'.

> **Ben Graham (1974)**

Ben Graham (in *The Intelligent Investor*) had quite long sets of criteria for the sort of stocks you would want to hold as a value investor. He even had separate screens for conservative investors, for whom a margin of safety was paramount, and for enterprising investors, who might be prepared to take some extra risk in the hope of higher returns. However, in those days, when a computer meant a person who performed calculations, you had to do it all by hand. Doubtless few except professional fund managers with rooms full of computers to do their bidding found the time.

The same computer revolution that paved the way for the efficient market hypothesis and the CAPM also allowed anyone with the knowledge and data access to screen large banks of data for companies that met the criteria they specified. One of the first to embrace the new technology was Benjamin Graham.

Graham's rules on stock filters changed throughout his life. The final version was published in *Forbes* magazine in 1977 shortly after his death. As he had extolled throughout his career, any investor could tilt the balance of risk and reward in their favour by finding cheap shares in companies that were profitable and financially sound. He identified ten factors that identified such companies. The filter was much simpler in operation than it looks, so bear with me.

## Graham's final formula

1. Earnings yield is more than twice the AAA bond yield.

2. P/E ratio is less than 40 per cent of the highest P/E the stock has had over the past five years.

3. Dividend yield is greater than two-thirds of the AAA corporate bond yield.

4. Price is less than two-thirds of tangible book value.

5. Price is less than two-thirds of net current asset value.

6. Total debt is less than book value.

7. Current assets greater than twice current liabilities.

8. Debt is less than twice net current assets.

9. Compound earnings growth is greater than 7 per cent over ten years.

10. Earnings declined more than 5 per cent no more than twice over the previous ten years.

The first five criteria determine value. Companies that exhibit these criteria are most likely to earn investors a high return in subsequent years. The second five criteria determine risk. Companies that pass these tests are least likely to falter and disappoint investors by not providing the expected returns. They provide the margin of safety that is such a central feature of Graham's writings.

This was more of a 'nice to have' list than a rigid take-it-or-leave-it stock filter that can be programmed into Excel, because very few companies meet all ten criteria. However Graham's research showed that a portfolio of shares that matched just two of the criteria, one from the first five, and one from the second, would do almost as well as all ten. The most important criteria were the first, a relatively high earnings yield (low P/E), and the sixth, a relatively low level of debt.

The reason Graham used the earnings yield is that he used as his benchmark for value the yield on top quality corporate bonds. Using earnings yield rather than the P/E allowed him to compare them directly. The corporate bonds of a company are always less risky than its shares, because if a company gets into trouble then bondholders are first in the queue for any payouts from the administrator and shareholders are at the back. Investors should therefore prefer bonds to shares unless the returns the shares offer are considerably better. This is why Graham looked for *twice* the return, i.e. an earnings yield of twice the AAA corporate bond yield – another application of his margin of safety.

When company profits fall, the companies most likely to fail completely are those with high levels of debt. Should a company fail completely there's no chance of a recovery, or of it ever paying investors the return they expected, so Graham was anxious to avoid the most indebted companies too.

Just using these two criteria together worked quite satisfactorily. From 1974 to 1981 the market averaged 14% per annum returns. But a portfolio of stocks that offered an earnings yield twice the AAA bond yield, and with total debt less than book value, would have had an annual return of 38%.[10]

Despite the complexity of his filter at first glance, Graham was in fact suggesting the same thing as Greenblatt and Piotroski are doing a generation later. Or rather, they are doing the same thing as he did: looking for companies with a downtrodden price but trying to minimise the risk that they will suddenly falter (i.e. value plus a margin of safety). The filter forces the buyer into a businesslike investment operation rather than speculating, another of Graham's favourite subjects.

---

[10] Oppenheimer, 1984.

# Chapter 16
## Joel Greenblatt: The P/E and Return on Capital

Joel Greenblatt is an American money manager. He started out emulating Benjamin Graham by setting up a partnership, Gotham Capital, in 1985. Gotham Capital invests in value shares and special situations such as mergers, spin-offs and bankruptcies. Greenblatt is also a professor on the adjunct faculty[11] at Columbia Business School, where Graham taught. He is very successful, having achieved annualised returns of 40% at Gotham from 1985 to 2005.

*The Little Book that Beats the Market* codifies his approach to value investing and has turned out to be an investment bestseller. Greenblatt's little book is not only minimalist in terms of its size (136 pages plus an appendix), but advocates a trading formula based on just two factors. The first is the earnings yield (the inverse of the P/E). The second is Return on Capital Employed. The combination of the two Greenblatt called his Magic Formula.

Greenblatt wrote his book as a parable to teach his children how to invest. He tells the story of Jason, a teenage entrepreneur who starts off buying packs of chewing gum each morning for 25c each. Then at school he sells each individual stick of chewing gum to his friends for 25c, the same as he had paid for the whole pack of five. Jason later goes on to open a chain of chewing-gum stores, each costing $400,000 to open, and making $200,000 profit every year. That 50% return on capital:

$$\frac{\text{profit}}{\text{capital employed}}$$

is an important factor in the valuation of Jason's company, Greenblatt says, because it means that every year his business can invest its profit in new chewing gum stores and compound its shareholders' money. A company making lower returns on its capital would have less money available for investment and therefore make lower profits for its investors in future.

Although a high return on capital one year does not guarantee a high return in subsequent years, on average Greenblatt's choices are more likely to have the opportunity to reinvest profit at a high rate.

---

[11] This is similar to a Visiting Professor in the UK. He might breeze in from time to time and deliver the odd lecture, but he's much too important to sit for weeks marking huge piles of exam papers. Unlike your author.

Greenblatt uses an unusual method to calculate earnings yield:

$$\frac{\text{EBIT}}{\text{enterprise value}} \quad \text{i.e.} \quad \frac{\text{earnings before interest and tax}}{\text{market value + net debt}}$$

This is similar to E/P, the inverse of the P/E, but viewing things at the company level rather than the per-share level. However, the earnings numerator excludes outgoings on paying interest and tax because these can differ so much among companies. The enterprise value denominator adds in net debt, because this is the total cost that somebody would have to take on if they wanted to acquire the company. Overall the ratio is designed to exclude the effect of different debt levels and tax rates, which can seriously distort P/E-based comparisons between companies.

Another slightly unusual route Greenblatt took was how he chose companies that had both a good return on capital and a high earnings yield. He ranked the largest 3500 US companies by return on capital, from 1 to 3500. He did the same for the earnings yield. Then he added the two ranks for each company together, so that companies with the best combination of return on capital and earnings yield formed his portfolios. Thus a company with an extraordinarily high return on capital, for example, could get away with having not quite so good an earnings yield and still make the cut.

These companies, he determined, were above average companies at below average prices. The book claims a back-tested average annual return of almost 31% for portfolios of the 30 or so top-ranked shares from 1998 to 2004, compared to the 12.3% average for all 3500 companies. Although the system lost money in a few individual years, it made money and beat the market over every three-year period.

The *Little Book* has wider significance too. Besides the reported investment success in back-tests, the book's folksy style and brevity have ensured it is widely read. If enough people read it and follow what it says, it should make the market more efficient. If investors buy shares as soon as they are mispriced, then the returns from them should fall. In effect the unloved companies of before will become more popular and command higher prices.

Greenblatt does not think that this will happen though, because the professional investors who now dominate the market could not live with sometimes years of underperformance revealed by Greenblatt's testing. As Warren Buffett says, the secret about value investing has been out there for 60 years (since *The Intelligent Investor* was published in 1949) but there still seems to be no shortage of extraordinarily mispriced value stocks.

# Chapter 17

## Joseph Piotroski: The P/E and the Fscore

In 2000 Joseph Piotroski was an associate professor of accounting at the University of Chicago. He noticed that the market-beating performance of value stocks, in particular companies selling at a low price-to-tangible book value (PTBV), depended on a minority of cheap companies that performed very strongly outweighing the weaker performance of the majority. He found that, after two years, only 44% of low PTBV companies beat the stock market average, although the group as a whole did.

One of the reasons why professional financial analysts rarely recommend the cheapest stocks even though, statistically speaking, they do well, may be this brutal reality: the chances of an individual value share beating the stock market over a two year period are less than 50:50.

Just like a low P/E ratio, a low PTBV is an indication that a share is unpopular and investors have been selling it, but it is a particularly conservative method of valuation because it discounts all future value that might be added by the company (profit in other words). Unlike the standard P/E ratio, it can still be used to value a company even when it is making a loss.

Often the shares are unpopular because profits are falling and investors see problems ahead, perhaps because the company lacks the financial resources to weather a difficult period. Fama and French believed that the risk associated with such companies explained their superior returns. An alternative explanation is that investors' fears are overdone and the share price of a typical low PTBV company has fallen below a realistic appraisal of the company's value. When the company begins to recover and publishes better results, its price rebounds sharply.

For Piotroski, the challenge was to weed out companies that were most likely to fail completely or suffer a prolonged period of sub-par profits from those that were temporarily distressed and more likely to make a rapid recovery. In the process he hoped to boost the already superior returns of low PTBV firms and improve the ratio of winners to losers.

To do that he turned to the information in the company's financial statements. The idea was to find companies that were financially strong from information in their income statements, balance sheets and cash flow accounts. He compiled nine signals to determine that a company was profitable, able to fund its operations and investment from its own profits, and could turn its assets into sales more efficiently.

Finances, and in particular the throughput of cash, are the lifeblood of any company. The indicators Piotroski chose are analogous to the biofunction monitor above each bed in the sick bay in the original *Star Trek* series. There are six vital signs that fluctuate up and down according to the health of the patient. Piotroski was looking to summarise the vital signs of a company. He found a huge difference in subsequent returns for the strongest and weakest companies, particularly for the smallest companies not covered by any analysts.

# How is the Fscore calculated?

I describe Piotroski's criteria below. It is simpler than in sick bay because each is a 0 or 1 indicator: the company either passes the test or it doesn't. They add up to give a score from 0 to 9. The sum of the nine indicators soon became known as the Fscore (for financial stability score), although Piotroski did not call it that in his original paper. If you want to avoid most of the accounting jargon, skip to the next section where this is all demonstrated as we work out Haynes' Fscore.

The components of the Fscore divide logically into three areas:

A.  Profitability

B.  Funding

C.  Efficiency

We'll look at each of these in turn.

## A. Profitability

Profitability measures provide evidence that companies are making money, which is obviously a prerequisite if investors are to benefit in the future.

1.  **Return on assets**: score 1 if positive, 0 if negative.

2.  **Change in return on assets to last year**: score 1 if it's higher, 0 if it's lower.

3.  **Net cash flow from operating activities**: score 1 if positive, 0 if negative.

4.  **Quality of earnings**: score 1 if cash flow > profit, 0 otherwise.

Companies where profits are driven by accruals (accounting decisions) typically earn lower returns than companies where profits were driven by rising levels of business. Struggling value companies might be tempted to massage their profits to avoid posting a loss, but (4) would penalise this.

## B. Funding

Funding measures provide evidence that a company can continue operating without having to borrow more or raise money from shareholders. Distressed low PTBV companies might find that banks are unwilling to lend them more money and shareholders may not want to invest.

5. **Change in gearing** (leverage): score 1 if gearing is lower, 0 if it's higher.

6. **Change in liquidity**: compare this year's current ratio (current assets divided by current liabilities) to last year's. Score 1 if this year's current ratio is higher, 0 if it's lower.

7. **Change in shares in issue**: score 1 provided the company has not issued any more shares this year, 0 otherwise.

The change in gearing checks to see whether the company's long-term funding position has improved. Liquidity looks at its short-term funding position. If a company has issued significant amounts of shares during the year, captured in the third signal, it probably did so to raise funds from investors. Like many of Piotroski's signals this wouldn't necessarily be a problem in a growing company, but for a company that is struggling it's a sign of weakness because it suggests the company is not earning enough profit to finance its business. It could also be a sign of desperation, because the company is selling its shares at a time when the price is low – precisely the wrong time to sell shares.

A relatively small increase in the number of shares in issue, for example to satisfy executive share options, may be permissible because it doesn't reflect financial weakness. Although Piotroski did not allow for this in his 2000 paper, in my retest I allowed a company to issue up to 10% new shares each year and still get a 1 for point (7).

## C. Efficiency

The final two signals, return on assets and asset turnover, measure changes in the efficiency of a business.

8.  **Change in gross margin**: score 1 if this year's gross margin is higher, 0 if it's lower.

9.  **Change in asset turnover**: score 1 if this year's asset turnover ratio (total sales divided by total assets at the beginning of the year) is higher, 0 if it's lower.

The gross profit margin measures how much of a company's sales remain as profit after deducting costs. Asset turnover relates a company's sales to the assets the company employs to produce those sales. If asset turnover increases, it means the company is using its assets more efficiently.

The more of these signals a company triggers, the stronger it is. A perfect score is nine out of nine, but nines and zeroes are very rare, as we shall see.

Piotroski did not claim to have chosen the best signals or that each signal deserved an equal weighting. He just picked a logical set and gave each signal the simplest weighting (bad or good), paving the way for investors to refine his or her system if they should choose to. The advantage of Piotroski's Fscore is that you don't need to have done A level maths to understand it.

# Example: Haynes' Fscore

All this accounting jargon will become a lot clearer if we look at Haynes' Fscore as at 1 May 2009. Note these are the DataStream figures so they may not be identical to those in the published financial statements.

## (1) Return on Assets (ROA)

$$ROA = \frac{\text{net income}}{\text{total assets}} = \frac{4,810,000}{52,127,000} = 9.23\%$$

*Positive, so score 1*

## (2) Change in ROA

2008 ROA was 11.13% but 2009 ROA is down to 9.23%.

*Negative, so score 0*

## (3) Cash flow from operating activities

+£7,192,000

*Positive, so score 1*

## (4) Quality of earnings (accruals)

7,192,000 > 4,810,000

*Positive, so score 1*

## (5) Change in gearing (leverage)

Haynes has no long-term debt in either year.

*Score 0 as gearing has not improved*

## (6) Change in liquidity

2008 current ratio was 3.29; 2009 current ratio is 4.39.

*Positive, so score 1*

## (7) Change in shares in issue

16,352,000 shares were in issue in both 2008 and 2009.

*Score 1 as there is the same number of shares in issue this year as last*

## (8) Change in gross margin

2008 gross margin was

$$\frac{\text{gross income}}{\text{sales}} = \frac{19,072,000}{31,122,000} = 61.28\%$$

2009 gross margin was:

$$\frac{\text{gross income}}{\text{sales}} = \frac{21,957,000}{35,335,000} = 62.14\%$$

*Score 1 as this year's gross margin is higher.*

## (9) Change in asset turnover

2008 asset turnover was:

$$\frac{\text{sales}}{\text{total assets}} = \frac{31,122,000}{45,281,000} = 68.73\%$$

2009 asset turnover was:

$$\frac{\text{sales}}{\text{total assets}} = \frac{35,355,000}{52,127,000} = 67.79\%$$

*Score 0 as this year's asset turnover ratio is lower.*

Haynes' Fscore for 2009 is therefore 6 out of 9, so good but not excellent.

## How well can the Fscore predict returns?

Piotroski took the lowest one-fifth of companies by PTBV and tested the Fscore to see how well it would predict the returns that were actually observed. Choosing companies with Fscores of eight or nine improved annual returns by 7.5% over the average. While only 32% of companies with low Fscores beat the market, 50% of the high Fscore companies went on to beat the market over one and two years. Companies with Fscores of zero or one were also five times more likely to delist than companies with high Fscores, leaving investors with nothing.

Smaller companies did best of all. Those with high Fscores earned annual returns *27% higher* on average than those with low Fscores. Although the Fscore is a financial stability indicator, not a value indicator, as an indicator of shares that are going to perform the Fscore does far better than PTBV, the P/E or any of the other value indicators.

The Fscore still worked well for medium-sized companies, but it was only marginally significant for the largest firms. Other factors that boosted the predictive power of the Fscore included low share turnover and no analyst following.

Piotroski reckoned the Fscore worked best on value shares because they tend to be overlooked by investors, particularly professional analysts who make forecasts and recommendations for fund managers. Since these companies are often suffering from some kind of financial distress, falling profits and a lack of funding, the information contained in the company's financial statements is more likely to be critical than for a growing company.

The Fscore works particularly well for small- and medium-sized value shares which are traded infrequently and do not have analysts following them. Only one-third of the companies in Piotroski's dataset had any analyst coverage at all, and of those that did the median number was only two analysts. Because unfashionable shares are neglected, the market is unpleasantly surprised when a company with a low Fscore fails or announces disappointing profits, and surprised in a nice way when a company with a high Fscore announces good profits. One of David Dreman's themes, in his academic papers as well as his 2012 book, is how often the market is surprised, and how bad it is at realising how often it is surprised.

A believer in efficient markets might reply that small, thinly traded companies about which there is little information are more risky investments. Piotroski says that doesn't seem realistic considering that the companies with the highest Fscores have the lowest financial and operating risk. I argued in Chapter 7 that Fama and French's identification of low PBV as a risk indicator seems more of an after-the-event justification. Saying that high Fscore companies are more risky makes even less sense. Piotroski purposely chose nine indicators that imply financial stability, and high Fscore companies are five times less likely to delist.

# The Fscore in the UK

There has been no peer-reviewed test of whether Piotroski's Fscore works as well in the UK, so I thought I would do the research for this book. Unfortunately a lot of the necessary company accounts information is not available on DataStream before 1995, so all these tests cover the 15 years from 1995 to 2010.

## The Fscore and price-to-tangible book value

Recall that Piotroski used only the lowest 20% of shares by PTBV in his paper (i.e. the value quintile). Table 12 on the other hand includes all companies with a book value, even those with a negative book value. You need to look at the Low PTBV row to get a comparison with Piotroski, although even that uses the lowest 1/3 of PTBV shares, not the lowest 1/5. The 'high minus low Fscore' figure there is 32.8%, so reasonably close to Piotroski's 27%.

Since we are interested in how the Fscore works with value indicators, the best way to test it is by doing a two-way sort: you arrange companies into a table, with one dimension the PTBV and the other dimension the Fscore, and calculate the average returns for the stocks that fall into each of the cells in that table: so what we would expect would give the best returns would be companies with an Fscore of 9 AND in the lowest PTBV decile. However, we need to be careful that we get enough companies in each cell group, bearing in mind that companies are not distributed across the ten possible Fscores evenly. In particular there are very few companies with Fscores of 0, 1 or 2. If we use deciles, or even quintiles, or fixed PTBV limits, then we end with some Fscore/PTBV groups having zero companies in them in a particular year, so we can't calculate the average return over our 15 years.

I spent the best part of two weeks messing around with this. The best compromise I could find was to sort companies into Fscores first, then within that group divide them equally into high, medium and low PTBV groups. This does however mean that the numerical values of the dividing lines between the low, medium and high PTBV cell buckets may well be different for, say, Fscore 3 compared to Fscore 9. I also had to group Fscores 0-2 together, again because some years there are very few or no companies that would fall into particular buckets otherwise.

**Table 12: Returns for high, medium and low price-to-book value groups within Fscores, 1995-2010**

| Fscore | 0-2 (Low) | 3 | 4 | 5 | 6 | 7 | 8 | 9 | 9 minus Low Fscore |
|---|---|---|---|---|---|---|---|---|---|
| High PTBV | -27.0% | -19.5% | -11.7% | 2.3% | 8.3% | 14.2% | 17.4% | 17.7% | 44.7% |
| Med PTBV | -20.2% | -8.5% | -0.1% | 4.0% | 8.9% | 17.2% | 22.2% | 20.1% | 40.3% |
| Low PTBV | -10.0% | -1.4% | 0.7% | 10.1% | 15.8% | 17.6% | 24.1% | 22.8% | 32.8% |
| Low - High PTBV | 17.0% | 18.1% | 12.4% | 7.8% | 7.5% | 3.4% | 6.7% | 5.1% | |

As Piotroski found in the US, there is a very wide difference in one-year returns between low and high F-score companies – much wider than any measure of the value-glamour split. However, this doesn't necessarily mean the market is as catastrophically inefficient as that 44.7% implies, because I am equally weighting companies, not weighting them by their market capitalisation. Journey Group at 3p has the same weight here as BP. Weighting companies by their market capitalisation, given that the FTSE 100 accounts for 80%+ of the total stock market value and valuations there are much more efficient, would doubtless much reduce the figures in the final column.

Looking at 'low – high PTBV' in the bottom row, it seems that price-to-book value works excellently with the weakest companies but doesn't tell us so much about the strongest. Companies with an Fscore of 0-2 and high PTBV returned a shocking -27% per annum over the 15 years. This could make sense (another *post hoc* rationalisation coming up) because if the company's life signs are deteriorating, a good wodge of tangible assets will give them something to fall back on, for a time, while they try to turn things around. If you have low or even negative tangible assets and your company's vital signs are getting worse then it could all soon be up for you.

On the other hand PTBV works far less well for the healthiest companies. If your life signs are all excellent and you are making healthy and growing profits then any tangible assets that you have are a necessary evil to support you in that process, nothing more. In fact PTBV works about as well as the traditional P/E for the strongest companies, and is outperformed by the ten-year and decomposed P/Es.

## The Fscore and the P/E

We now move on to something that Piotroski never looked at in his 2000 paper. How does the Fscore work with the P/E as the value indicator, as opposed to PTBV? Fewer companies have a P/E than a PTBV, because quite a few companies might be making losses in any one year, but most companies have at least some tangible assets. Because of this I had to group Fscores 0-4 and 8-9 together. Some years there are very few or no companies that would fall into particular buckets otherwise.

So that we can compare Table 13, Table 14 and Table 15 together, Table 13 includes only companies with a ten-year history of positive earnings. However it uses the traditional P/E to assign companies to buckets.

**Table 13: Returns for high, medium and low *traditional* P/E groups within Fscores, all companies with ten or more years of positive earnings, 1995-2010**

| Fscore | 0-4 (Low) | 5 | 6 | 7 | 8-9 (High) | High minus Low Fscore |
|---|---|---|---|---|---|---|
| High P/E | 1.6% | 4.0% | 9.0% | 12.0% | 17.0% | 15.4% |
| Medium P/E | -1.4% | 5.5% | 8.3% | 12.3% | 16.6% | 17.4% |
| Low P/E | -0.7% | 6.0% | 9.7% | 16.3% | 19.0% | 19.7% |
| Low - High P/E | -2.3% | 2.0% | 0.7% | 4.3% | 2.0% | |

So the traditional P/E just about works for the most financially stable companies (19% versus 17% in the high Fscore column) but it would work *against* us if we were investing in the least stable companies (-0.7% versus 1.6% in the low Fscore column).

By far the most powerful effect comes from sorting by Fscore, not by P/E (15% to 19% in the right-hand column, versus 2% to 4% in the bottom row). Looking at these results it's not surprising that the P/E has fallen by the wayside in recent years.

The troubling figure here is that -2.3% for the weakest companies. I could try to dismiss it as possibly due to random statistical variation, but if you look below, the long-term and decomposed P/Es also work the opposite way round to normal for the weakest companies. I don't know why weak companies with high P/Es should do better than weak companies with low P/Es. This, as they say, is a subject for future research.

On to the ten-year and decomposed P/Es:

**Table 14: Returns for high, medium and low *ten-year* P/E groups within Fscores, all companies with ten or more years of positive earnings, 1995-2010**

| Fscore | 0-4 (Low) | 5 | 6 | 7 | 8-9 (High) | High minus Low Fscore |
|---|---|---|---|---|---|---|
| High P/E | 4.7% | 2.5% | 7.5% | 11.7% | 13.0% | 8.3% |
| Medium P/E | -2.8% | 6.6% | 10.7% | 14.1% | 19.7% | 22.5% |
| Low P/E | -2.5% | 6.6% | 8.1% | 15.0% | 19.7% | 22.3% |
| Low - High P/E | -7.2% | 4.1% | 0.6% | 3.3% | 6.7% | |

Now the ten-year P/E gives a reasonable discrimination between value and glamour firms for the strongest companies (19.7% versus 13% in the high Fscore column) – about the same as the 5% to 6% difference in high and low PTBV companies for high Fscore companies (Table 12, bottom column, rightmost two cells).

For the decomposed P/E:

**Table 15: Returns for high, medium and low *decomposed* P/E groups within Fscores, all companies with ten or more years of positive earnings, 1995-2010**

| Fscore | 0-4 (Low) | 5 | 6 | 7 | 8-9 (High) | High minus Low Fscore |
|---|---|---|---|---|---|---|
| High P/E | -0.1% | 2.6% | 4.8% | 10.3% | 14.3% | 14.4% |
| Medium P/E | 1.7% | 6.6% | 7.3% | 14.3% | 14.9% | 13.2% |
| Low P/E | -2.3% | 7.1% | 14.4% | 16.2% | 22.9% | 25.2% |
| Low - High P/E | -2.2% | 4.5% | 9.6% | 5.9% | 8.6% | |

So the decomposed P/E works quite respectably for the strongest companies (22.9% versus 14.3% in the high Fscore column), and with a difference between high and low decomposed P/Es of 8.6% (high Fscore column, bottom cell) is more powerful at identifying value firms within that group than PTBV (Table 12, bottom column, rightmost two cells).

And finally to the Naked P/E. Chapter 13 used very small portfolios of a few shares, so I do the same here, but restrict the companies that may be chosen to those with

Fscores of 8 or 9 for the value shares, and Fscores of 0 to 3 for the glamour group. We can afford to be highly selective here because we are investing in so few companies each year.

**Figure 16: Combining the Naked P/E with Fscores. All UK companies 1975-2010 (Fscore from 1995)**

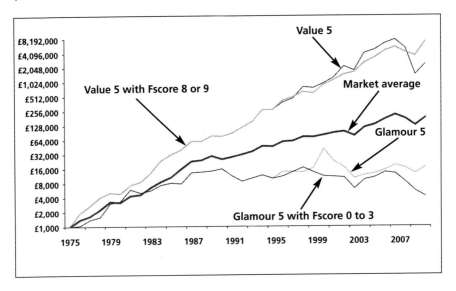

Note that the lines only diverge from 1995 onwards because that is when I could first get all the accounting statistics from DataStream. Investing in only the most financially sound companies underperforms for most of the time compared to using the Naked P/E on its own, but importantly it does protect us in hard times. Using it we would have largely avoided the -72% catastrophe the Naked P/E on its own suffered in 2008-9. The companies with Fscores of 8 or 9 suffered only a 16% loss in that year. We would have protected our portfolio worth £7m having stuck to high Fscore shares, compared to a drop down to £2.4m using the Naked P/E alone.

Glamour shares performed much worse, as we would expect for Fscores 0-3, and end up worth £4000 compared to £17,000 if we don't take account of the Fscore. These weakest companies didn't even participate in the 1999-2000 technology stock bubble, falling by 18% in 1999-2000 compared to +150% growth for the original glamour portfolio.

# Going beyond the P/E

So how can we summarise the results of combining Piotroski's Fscore with value indicators?

The most important lesson to draw is that the Fscore is a very powerful indicator of future returns. You could do a lot worse than simply buy a random portfolio of companies with Fscores of 8 or 9 and forget about value measures altogether.

Clearly the market is *not* fully taking into account the information held in the published financial reports, although it does this better for larger companies with more analysts following them. The almost 50% difference in annual returns for Fscore 2/high PTBV versus Fscore 9/low PTBV portfolios should be proof enough of market inefficiency.

The P/E is of little use if you want to identify glamour companies that will perform poorly. Use PTBV instead.

For value investors buying large portfolios of low P/E companies, combining the Fscore with the decomposed P/E works best out of all the P/E measures we have surveyed.

For enterprising investors who are prepared to accept a concentrated portfolio, the Naked P/E remains a very powerful value indicator. Most usefully, combining it with only buying high Fscore companies saves us from disaster when the market as a whole is in a bad state.

These results show that there is more to value than one measure. Profitability ratios and balance sheet ratios such as gearing are excellent predictors of returns when combined with value measures, either PTBV or the P/E measures developed in this book. In other words, it is not only possible but desirable to go beyond the P/E.

# Conclusion

In a short book we have been on a long journey, from how earnings are calculated, to splitting out the components of the P/E and combining them in a stock filter with Piotroski's Fscore.

Here I try to summarise the most important lessons. Many of them are about the stock market and value shares in general, not just about the P/E. I also give a few pointers to how this work might be taken forward in the future.

## What have we learnt? Market efficiency and the value premium

- Even confirmed value investors agree that the market is mostly efficient, most of the time, at least for larger stocks. If the market were fully efficient, Warren Buffett would be 'a bum on the street with a tin cup', as he puts it, not one of the richest men in the world. Where believers in efficient markets part company with value investors is in the extent of the mispricing. The former feel it is so minor and short-term as not to be worth worrying about; the latter feel that the mispricing is quite widespread and can persist for years.

- Contrary to what most people outside the investment world think, the stock market is not a lottery either. If prices really were random then there would be no profit for value investors to take, because there would be no fair value price to which their shares would eventually move to. Warren Buffett would be out on the street again.

- Most of the mispricing can be found in smaller stocks, particularly those quoted on AIM in the UK. Companies on AIM have less exacting reporting standards, and companies with a market capitalisation of less than £50m will have few if any analysts following them. It is with these companies that private investors prepared to get their hands dirty reading annual reports could really make their mark. That Buffett now considers any company worth less than $5bn not worth his time analysing emphasises his achievement and shows how far up the scale the mispricing spreads.

- Both sides of the academic debate agree that value shares perform better in the long term than the market, which in turn outperforms glamour shares. What there is no agreement on is whether value shares are riskier. In an efficient market there should be no free lunch, and a willingness to take on extra risk should be the down payment for higher returns. If value shares really are more risky, what that extra riskiness in fact is has proved difficult to pin down.

- Don't trust earnings forecasts. It has been known since 1962 that accurate earnings forecasts are difficult if not impossible to make, but the market seems uniquely unable to take this fact into account. Systems such as the PEG that rely on earnings forecasts are likely to prove no more successful than systems that rely on historic earnings.

## What have we learnt? The P/E

- Taking into account several past years of earnings, as suggested by Graham and Dodd in 1934 but not tested for 70 years, does indeed give a more reliable view of a company's long-term earning power. The long-term P/E increases the power of the traditional P/E to predict returns by two-thirds.

- The P/E as currently formulated is a rag-bag of different influences with widely differing powers to predict returns. In particular, the sector effect, wrapped up as it is in the traditional P/E, is working against the others. Companies in high P/E sectors do perform better than those in low P/E sectors. This is not a very strong effect, but it is statistically significant. Splitting out these influences, weighting them according to their ability to predict returns and putting them back together again results in a yet more powerful 'decomposed P/E'.

- The improved P/E's main defect is that it is by design a long-term, backward-looking measure. It can take no account of whether the company has got into difficulties recently. This was graphically demonstrated by the catastrophic returns to the Naked P/E portfolio in 2008-9.

- Luckily, combining an earnings-based value measure with a measure of a company's current financial stability can mostly avoid this problem. Other successful investors have done this in the past with varying methods. The Naked P/E combined with Piotroski's Fscore showed some outstanding results and mostly avoided the 2008-9 collapse.

# What remains to be learned?

Academic papers traditionally end with a list of questions that the work has thrown up. This helps future researchers immeasurably in their never-ending search for topics for research. This book will continue that tradition; I hope you will find the questions thought-provoking.

- Different components of earnings probably have different powers to predict returns. A start has been made here with Tony Kang's work on using operating income as the denominator in the P/E. Effectively he weighted items high up in the profit and loss account with a '1' and everything below operating income with a '0'. We could become a lot more sophisticated in how we weight the different components of earnings according to their power to predict returns. This would be meaningless to accountants but could be of great use to investors.

- My MSc dissertation used only five years of past earnings, and I found a slight but significant improvement in the power of the P/E. My PhD work went back eight years and much improved its power. Updating my published papers for this book, I went back ten years and the extra years still seemed to be adding more information. How far back does this go? Are Haynes' earnings from 31 years ago (for they have made a profit every year since then) also going to add power to their P/E as a predictor of their returns? This seems against common sense, but as we have seen with predicting earnings and the PEG, common sense can lead you up blind alleys if you ignore the statistical evidence. So-called 'long memory' systems are common in finance and elsewhere, but no-one has yet demonstrated them at the level of individual companies.

- Dividing (today's share price) by (individual one-year earnings from six or more years ago) gives a P/E that is *more powerful* than the traditional P/E. This too is against the common-sense notion that last year's earnings should tell us the most about a company's true earnings potential. What is muddying the waters to make last year's earnings, and indeed those from two and three years ago, less useful?

- The components of the P/E that I separated out are far from the final truth on the matter. The Naked P/E probably includes other predictable factors that I simply haven't thought of. One I have thought of, but not included yet, is gearing: other things being equal, a company with more debt should expect a lower P/E because it is more risky.

- Why do all these developments of the P/E work the 'wrong way round' to normal, i.e. high P/E companies give better subsequent returns than low P/E companies, when used on the financially weakest companies?

## A final word about the value premium

Don't be afraid to exploit it to the hilt, and don't be afraid that it will disappear. The secret has been out for 60 years now since *The Intelligent Investor* was published, and there is no evidence of the value premium disappearing. If you are truly able to switch off your emotions and invest according to the statistics and nothing else, you will be one of the handful of value investors in the market, afloat on a sea of euphoria and fear.

# Appendices

# FTSE 100 EPSs and P/Es

This appendix shows EPS and P/E figures for all companies in the FTSE 100 Index as at 21 February 2012. Where PE10 is not shown, either the company's earnings are not stated in pounds sterling, or less than ten years of earnings are available. All data are from DataStream.

| Name | Price(p) | EPS | Hist.P/E | Hist.P/E10 | Forecast P/E |
|---|---|---|---|---|---|
| ADMIRAL GROUP | 1043 | 81.9 | 12.7 | | 13.2 |
| AGGREKO | 2168 | 78.57 | 27.6 | 65.9 | 25.1 |
| AMEC | 1111 | 71.9 | 15.5 | 28.5 | 16.4 |
| ANGLO AMERICAN | 2715.5 | 5.06 | 8.5 | | 8.9 |
| ANTOFAGASTA | 1326 | 79.98 | 16.6 | 27.3 | 16.3 |
| ARM HOLDINGS | 582 | 12.45 | 46.7 | 112.4 | 41.6 |
| ASHMORE GROUP | 389.3 | 28.08 | 13.9 | | 16.2 |
| ASSOCIATED BRIT.FOODS | 1223 | 73.76 | 16.6 | 22.5 | 14.2 |
| ASTRAZENECA | 2841.5 | 462.21 | 6.1 | 12.2 | 7.4 |
| AVIVA | 375.6 | 77.3 | 4.9 | 5.3 | 7.2 |
| BAE SYSTEMS | 320.6 | 45.5 | 7 | 10.9 | 7.8 |
| BARCLAYS | 247.75 | 25.1 | 9.9 | 5.5 | 8.3 |
| BG GROUP | 1480.5 | 82.75 | 17.9 | 29.8 | 16.2 |
| BHP BILLITON | 2080 | 4.27 | 7.7 | | 8.5 |
| BP | 497.7 | 135.93 | 3.7 | 10.1 | 7.1 |
| BRITISH AMERICAN TOBACCO | 3114 | 173.7 | 17.9 | 30.2 | 16.1 |
| BRITISH LAND | 477.3 | 29.4 | 16.2 | 14.7 | 16.3 |
| BRITISH SKY BCAST.GROUP | 690 | 45.6 | 15.1 | 26.4 | 14.1 |
| BT GROUP | 216 | 23 | 9.4 | 11.0 | 9.5 |
| BUNZL | 908.5 | 64.18 | 14.2 | 21.3 | 13.8 |
| BURBERRY GROUP | 1439 | 55.7 | 25.8 | 51.4 | 23.3 |
| CAIRN ENERGY | 347 | 0 | | 102.9 | 5 |
| CAPITA | 646.5 | 46.59 | 13.9 | 25.4 | 13.7 |
| CAPITAL SHOPCTS.GROUP | 339.9 | 20.61 | 16.5 | 15.8 | 21.1 |
| CARNIVAL | 1942 | 2.43 | 12.7 | | 15.2 |
| CENTRICA | 295.7 | 20.91 | 14.1 | 15.7 | 11.6 |
| COMPASS GROUP | 630 | 39 | 16.2 | 26.8 | 14.9 |
| CRH | 1360 | 0.69 | 23.4 | | 21.4 |
| DIAGEO | 1483.5 | 76.29 | 19.4 | 24.9 | 16.3 |
| ESSAR ENERGY | 123 | 13.22 | 9.3 | | 11.4 |
| EURASIAN NATRES.CORP. | 723 | 1.91 | 6.3 | | 6.9 |
| EVRAZ | 412.7 | | | | 11.4 |

| Name | Price(p) | EPS | Hist.P/E | Hist.P/E10 | Forecast P/E |
|------|---------|-----|----------|------------|--------------|
| EXPERIAN | 942 | 0.7 | 21.2 | | 18.9 |
| FRESNILLO | 1750 | 1.04 | 27.5 | | 21.6 |
| G4S | 278.6 | 22.3 | 12.5 | 20.7 | 12.2 |
| GKN | 225.5 | 19.9 | 11.3 | 11.3 | 10.4 |
| GLAXOSMITHKLINE | 1413 | 114.1 | 12.4 | 15.9 | 11.5 |
| GLENCORE INTERNATIONAL | 438.35 | | | | 11 |
| HAMMERSON | 395.9 | 19.8 | 20 | 18.5 | 20.3 |
| HARGREAVES LANSDOWN | 481.5 | 22.5 | 21.4 | | 20.4 |
| HSBC HDG. (ORD $0.50) | 579.5 | 56.49 | 10.3 | 11.2 | 10.7 |
| ICAP | 395.8 | 38.7 | 10.2 | 15.0 | 10.6 |
| ICTL.HTLS.GP. | 1423 | 82.67 | 17.2 | | 17.5 |
| IMI | 966 | 74.4 | 13 | 24.2 | 12.4 |
| IMPERIAL TOBACCO GP. | 2481 | 188 | 13.2 | 20.5 | 12.2 |
| INTERNATIONAL POWER | 336.2 | 27.9 | 12.1 | 15.8 | 12.9 |
| INTERTEK GROUP | 2238 | 89 | 25.1 | 45.2 | 21.5 |
| INTL.CONS.AIRL.GP.(CDI) | 169.9 | | | | 13.7 |
| ITV | 79.55 | 8.3 | 9.6 | 15.3 | 11.3 |
| JOHNSON MATTHEY | 2333 | 135.5 | 17.2 | 28.1 | 16.6 |
| KAZAKHMYS | 1163 | 2.97 | 6.1 | | 6.3 |
| KINGFISHER | 277.5 | 22.91 | 12.1 | 16.5 | 11.4 |
| LAND SECURITIES GROUP | 683 | 39.25 | 17.4 | 12.6 | 17.7 |
| LEGAL & GENERAL | 121.8 | 0 | | 13.4 | 9.3 |
| LLOYDS BANKING GROUP | 35.75 | 0 | | 1.9 | 14.3 |
| MAN GROUP | 134.8 | 7.64 | 17.6 | 5.7 | 17.3 |
| MARKS & SPENCER GROUP | 354.9 | 33.8 | 10.5 | 11.6 | 10.6 |
| MEGGITT | 380.7 | 29.9 | 12.7 | 19.9 | 12.4 |
| MORRISON(WM)SPMKTS. | 295 | 24.08 | 12.3 | 22.1 | 11.7 |
| NATIONAL GRID | 643.5 | 50.68 | 12.7 | 15.9 | 13.1 |
| NEXT | 2767 | 233 | 11.9 | 19.4 | 11.6 |
| OLD MUTUAL | 158 | 17.2 | 9.2 | 12.1 | 8.7 |
| PEARSON | 1218 | 77.7 | 15.7 | 26.4 | 14.5 |
| PETROFAC | 1566 | 1.32 | 19.5 | | 16.3 |
| POLYMETAL INTERNATIONAL | 1045 | | | | 14.4 |
| PRUDENTIAL | 715.5 | 73.2 | 9.8 | 13.1 | 12.5 |
| RANDGOLD RESOURCES | 7135 | 4.13 | 27.3 | | 17.1 |

| Name | Price(p) | EPS | Hist.P/E | Hist.P/E10 | Forecast P/E |
|---|---|---|---|---|---|
| RECKITT BENCKISER GROUP | 3578 | 249.9 | 14.3 | 26.0 | 14.6 |
| REED ELSEVIER | 550.5 | 46.83 | 11.8 | 14.7 | 11.2 |
| RESOLUTION | 260.8 | 479.38 | 0.5 | | 8.5 |
| REXAM | 384.4 | 34.29 | 11.2 | 12.2 | 10.8 |
| RIO TINTO | 3699.5 | 442.64 | 8.4 | 15.5 | 7.3 |
| ROLLS-ROYCE HOLDINGS | 799 | 48.54 | 16.5 | 29.8 | 14.6 |
| ROYAL BANK OF SCTL.GP. | 28.21 | 0 | | 0.8 | 15.5 |
| ROYAL DUTCH SHELL A(LON) | 2303.5 | 356.3 | 7.8 | | 8 |
| ROYAL DUTCH SHELL B | 2333.5 | 290.7 | 8 | 12.4 | 8.3 |
| RSA INSURANCE GROUP | 113.6 | 11.3 | 10.1 | 11.5 | 8.1 |
| SABMILLER | 2544 | 1.7 | 23.7 | | 19.7 |
| SAGE GROUP | 305.6 | 20.81 | 14.7 | 22.9 | 14.7 |
| SAINSBURY (J) | 306 | 27.27 | 11.2 | 15.5 | 11.3 |
| SCHRODERS | 1598 | 123.1 | 13 | 28.3 | 14.7 |
| SCHRODERS NV | 1273 | 49.3 | 25.8 | 26.2 | |
| SERCO GROUP | 540 | 36.9 | 14.6 | 27.9 | 14.3 |
| SEVERN TRENT | 1528 | 104.59 | 14.6 | 18.2 | 17.6 |
| SHIRE | 2225 | 87.74 | 25.4 | 52.7 | 17.3 |
| SMITH & NEPHEW | 626.5 | 74.5 | 8.4 | 19.0 | 13 |
| SMITHS GROUP | 1047 | 92.7 | 11.3 | 16.7 | 11.5 |
| SSE | 1291 | 104.2 | 12.4 | 15.6 | 11.7 |
| STANDARD CHARTERED | 1641.5 | 123.4 | 13.3 | 21.2 | 13.1 |
| STANDARD LIFE | 233.9 | 25 | 9.4 | | 14.8 |
| TATE & LYLE | 699 | 54.9 | 12.7 | 18.0 | 12.7 |
| TESCO | 322.7 | 33.1 | 9.7 | 13.8 | 9.4 |
| TULLOW OIL | 1543 | 19.22 | 80.3 | 144.6 | 33.6 |
| UNILEVER (UK) | 2076 | 126.12 | 16.5 | 19.6 | 15.3 |
| UNITED UTILITIES GROUP | 599.5 | 34.6 | 17.3 | 12.6 | 16.9 |
| VEDANTA RESOURCES | 1453 | 158.86 | 9.1 | | 11.9 |
| VODAFONE GROUP | 175.8 | 15.78 | 11.1 | 14.6 | 11.1 |
| WEIR GROUP | 2152 | 106 | 20.3 | 48.3 | 16.6 |
| WHITBREAD | 1706 | 116.52 | 14.6 | 22.6 | 13 |
| WOLSELEY | 2419 | 142.9 | 16.9 | 10.1 | 15.3 |
| WPP | 799.5 | 63.2 | 12.7 | 19.2 | 12.3 |
| XSTRATA | 1210 | 1.97 | 9.7 | | 10 |

# Glossary

### amortisation

The process of reducing a company's goodwill over the years. Analogous to depreciation, but amortisation is only applied to intangible assets.

### APT

See Arbitrage Pricing Theory.

### Arbitrage Pricing Theory (APT)

Proposed by Ross in 1976, APT proposes a multi-dimensional view of risk, as opposed to the CAPM's one-dimensional view. The real world consists of multiple sources of risk and a company has its own sensitivities to each source. For example, a highly indebted chain of PC retailers will be very sensitive to rises in interest rates, but a traditional manufacturing company that owns most of its own assets will be much less sensitive. As for the CAPM, once the risk sources and sensitivities are known, expected returns can be calculated for the share. The APT as originally proposed is a general framework and does not specify what the sources of risk are.

### assets

What a company owns. Assets are recorded in a company's balance sheet. Haynes' biggest category of assets is intangible assets, the accounting value of its trademarks, know-how, computer software it has developed, and goodwill. These are not physical items, like the offices, workshops, tools and vehicles that comprise its second biggest category of asset (property plant and equipment) but their value can be included in the balance sheet if the company can identify the asset and assign a value to it. For example, software is included at the cost of developing it, and goodwill is the amount Haynes paid when it bought other companies, over the value of their physical assets. In other words, when a company buys another company the price it pays establishes the value of its intangible assets. Intangible assets and property, plant and equipment are examples of fixed assets, which have a useful life of over one year. Current assets will probably be used within a year. They include cash, money owed by customers (trade and other receivables), and stock (inventories) that will be sold. All of these assets are necessary so that the company can make a profit and pay its bills.

## balance sheet

One of a company's financial statements. It shows what the company owns, its assets, and what the company owes, its liabilities. The difference belongs to shareholders. This is shareholders' equity, also recorded in the balance sheet.

## beta

Beta is the sensitivity of a share's price movements to those of the market as a whole. So a beta of 2.0 means that if the market goes up or down by 5%, then you would expect the share to go up or down by 10%. Technically, beta is the slope of the regression of company returns against market returns. Typically, monthly returns over the past five years are used in the calculation. Different betas will result if different market proxies (FTSE 100, 350 or All-share) or different time periods are used. Under the CAPM returns must be proportional to the beta of a share.

The best way of explaining beta I have come across is: plot a scatter chart of returns on the market versus returns on a share. Draw a line of best fit. The slope of that line is the share's beta. Students or academics who want to calculate beta themselves can do this themselves even in Excel by using the SLOPE function, which gives the slope of a regression line between two variables.

## book value

The current value of assets on the balance sheet, after depreciation (tangible assets) or amortisation (intangible assets).

## Capital Asset Pricing Model (CAPM)

Under a set of restrictive assumptions assuming a perfectly efficient market, Sharpe's 1964 CAPM is a mathematical proof that returns on a share must be proportional to that share's riskiness compared to the market (i.e. its beta). The applicability of Sharpe's assumptions to the real world is questionable. Related models such as the Intertemporal CAPM and Consumption CAPM have since been suggested, but because the CAPM calculation gives an easily derived cost of capital, the original CAPM is still widely assumed to be true in many real world corporate finance decisions.

## CAPM

See Capital Asset Pricing Model.

## company year

Companies have their own year end. UK Listing Authority rules state that preliminary accounts should be filed within 120 days of this year end. In the US most companies have a year end of 31 December (and so for convenience academic papers using US data usually ignore companies that don't), but in the UK company year ends are distributed throughout the year.

## diluted earnings per share

Diluted earnings per share is an adjustment to basic earnings per share that accounts for potential shares outstanding in the year, for example share options awarded to employees or convertible bonds. When an employee exercises his options, or a bond is converted to shares, the number of shares in issue will increase, spreading the company's profits more thinly. However, depending on the agreement the company struck with employees and bond holders, the company may receive money from them for exercising the options or converting the bonds and profits may increase if, say, the company's interest bill falls due to interest on the bonds no longer being payable. Where the dilutive effect of the increased number of shares outweighs any increase in profit, it is recorded in diluted earnings per share, a measure of the company's performance preferred by prudent investors.

## dividend

Dividends are payments made by companies to their owners. They are the only returns shareholders receive unless they sell their shares. In the US dividends are typically paid as four equal quarterly amounts. In the UK they are paid half-yearly, usually as a 1/3 interim dividend and a 2/3 final dividend. Although many companies don't pay dividends, people will still invest in them in anticipation of dividends in the future. To pay dividends, a company must first earn profit, some of which it will retain to pay for expansion, or keep as a cushion in difficult years. The rest it pays to its shareholders.

## dividend yield (DY)

The dividend yield measures the annual return investors receive from dividend payments expressed as a percentage of the share price. To calculate the dividend yield, divide the per-share value of all the interim dividends paid by the company in the financial year and the final dividend proposed in its annual report by the current share price, and express it as a percentage:

dividend yield = total dividend (per share)/current share price X 100

The dividend can be directly compared to the running yield on a bond or the interest rate on a savings account. Any DY quoted will either be historic, using the sum of the interim and final dividends paid in the last company year, or prospective, using a forecast for total dividends to be paid in the current company year. One drawback of the dividend yield is it only measures the income from a shareholding, and not capital gains.

## DY

See dividend yield.

## earnings

Earnings are the net profit earned by a company in a year, after deducting the costs of production (cost of sales), distribution costs, administrative costs, interest payments and tax from the company's sales. It is the profit that remains for investors, paid to them as dividends and/or retained in the business to fund its activities. The earnings figure doesn't account for unrealised losses, or gains, which are recorded in the consolidated statement of changes in equity.

## earnings per share

Earnings per share is the company's earnings for a period, usually a year or half-year divided by the weighted average number of shares in issue during that period:

earnings per share = earnings/weighted average number of shares in issue

Knowing a company's earnings per share allows an investor to calculate how much of a company's profit is attributable to them, and whether that number has increased or decreased since previous years. By dividing the price of a company (per share) to its earnings per share he or she can calculate the company's price-earnings ratio

(P/E). EPS is either historic EPS (earnings in the last company year, as quoted in the annual report) or prospective EPS (a forecast for EPS in the current company year).

## earnings yield

The reciprocal of the P/E, i.e. earnings divided by price (E/P) rather than price divided by earnings. Widely used in academic papers because of the nasty discontinuity the P/E suffers as earnings go through zero.

## glamour shares

Glamour shares typically have a high P/E, high price to tangible book value or low dividend yield. If you sort shares by any of these statistics, the glamour shares will be concentrated at the opposite end of the sort order to the value shares. Academic research shows that such shares under-perform the market on average over the long-term, but there is no agreement on whether they are fundamentally less risky. These shares are typically exciting companies that are often in the news, and being able to talk knowledgeably about them will gain you considerable credibility at dinner parties.

## goodwill

An accountant's term to cover what a company has paid in a takeover over and above the tangible assets of the target firm. This may be fair value for estimates of the value of their intellectual property rights and customers' brand loyalty, but often it is simply a record of how much the bidder overpaid in order to effect the takeover. Goodwill has to be amortised over future years.

## gross profit

Gross profit is the first measure of profit listed on the income statement. It is revenues minus cost of sales. Since it ignores other administrative and distribution costs, interest and tax, it is far removed from the earnings or profit attributable to shareholders.

## income statement

Also known as the profit and loss account. The income statement tells us how much profit a company made in a period of time, usually a year or half-year, which is its net profit or earnings after deducting the costs of producing and selling its product or service from its revenues. The income statement doesn't include unrealised profits, which are recorded in the consolidated statement of changes in equity.

## intangible assets

Everything listed in a company's accounts that you can't in principle touch. This includes intellectual property rights and brand loyalty from customers.

## net profit

See earnings.

## operating profit

Operating profit is money earned by the company after deducting the costs of production, administration and distribution. It is one of the main measures of profit, often used to calculate profit margins and compare one business to another. Operating profit does not account for taxation and interest.

## payout ratio

Although a company's net profit belongs to shareholders, companies don't usually pay it all out as dividends. The company will keep some of the profit to fund its growth, and act as a cushion in difficult times. The proportion of net profit that the company pays out in dividends is the payout ratio. Some companies (typically regulated utilities such as water and electricity companies) that have limited prospects for growth have very high payout ratios. Other companies such as young technology companies will retain most of their profit to invest in developing their products and services. The payout ratio is the dividend per share expressed as a percentage of the earnings per share:

$$\text{payout ratio} = \frac{\text{DPS}}{\text{EPS}} \times 100\%$$

Haynes has a payout ratio of about 50%.

**PBV**

See price-to-book value.

**PCF**

See price-to-cash flow.

**P/E or PE**

See price/earnings ratio.

### price-to-book value (PBV)

The current share price divided by the total assets per share. A value company would typically have PBV less than 1.0 (i.e. the company's market capitalisation is less than the book value of its assets).

### price-to-cash flow (PCF)

The current share price divided by the cash flow per share. Another value indicator, with a low PCF preferred.

### price-to-sales ratio (PSR)

The current market capitalisation divided by the total sales in the last company year, as given in the company accounts. A value company would typically have PSR less than 1.0, i.e. the company's market capitalisation is less than last year's sales, but this depends very much on the industry the company is operating in.

### price-to-tangible book value (PTBV)

As price-to-book value but ignoring intangible assets such as intellectual rights or customer goodwill.

### price/earnings ratio (PE or P/E)

The share price divided by the EPS. The P/E quoted is either the historic P/E (share price divided by the EPS in the last company year, as quoted in the annual report) or the prospective P/E (share price divided by the average of analysts' forecasts for EPS in the current company year).

## profit attributable to shareholders/equity holders

See earnings.

## profit and loss account

See income statement.

## PSR

See price-to-sales ratio.

## PTBV

See price-to-tangible book value.

## retained earnings/profit

Retained earnings can refer to the profit retained by the company in an accounting period, after it has paid shareholders a dividend (see earnings). It can also refer to the cumulative total of the profit (and loss) it has retained year after year since it was formed, which is recorded in the balance sheet. There it can also be known as the 'share premium fund' (see shareholders' funds). Retained profits are a source of funding for the company, that should, if invested wisely, increase its profits in future.

## revenue

'Revenue' is another word for 'sales'. It is the company's income before any costs are deducted.

## risk

See volatility.

## tangible assets

The things a company owns that you can in principle touch – even cash in bank accounts if you withdrew it.

## value investor

A man (I have never heard of a female value investor but would be glad to be corrected) who uses investment ratios, such as the P/E or PTBV, to identify stocks that he believes are undervalued and so hopes to beat the market in the medium term (2-3 years).

## value premium

The superior performance value shares give in the long-term. For the P/E in the US and UK this is typically 3% per annum over average stock market returns.

## value shares

Shares selected using some ratio favoured by value investors such as low P/E, low PTBV or high DY. If you sort shares by any of these statistics, the value shares will be concentrated at the opposite end of the sort order to the glamour shares. Academic research shows that such shares outperform the market on average over the long-term, but there is no agreement on whether such shares are fundamentally more risky. Such shares are typically boring companies or even those that have been in trouble recently.

## volatility

The standard deviation of daily returns on a share. This is usually what is termed by researchers in academic finance as 'risk' because it is easily calculated, but it does not correspond to an everyday understanding of risk, e.g. 'The risk that this company will go bankrupt' or 'The risk that this investment will not provide me with an income equal to the national median wage at retirement'.

## weighted average shares in issue

The weighted average number of shares in issue is used to calculate earnings per share. Since companies can issue new shares or cancel existing ones, the total number of shares in issue at the end of an accounting period is not necessarily representative of the total number in issue throughout the period in which the company made a profit or loss. The weighted average accounts for shares only in proportion to that part of the year in which they were issued.

# References

Anderson, K. and Brooks, C. 2006. *The Long-Term Price-Earnings Ratio*, Journal of Business Finance and Accounting, 33(7/8): 1063-1086.

Anderson, K. and Brooks, C. 2006. *Decomposing the Price-Earnings Ratio*, Journal of Asset Management, 6(6): 456-469.

Anderson, K. and Brooks, C. 2007. *Extreme Returns from Extreme Value Stocks: Enhancing the Value Premium*, Journal of Investing, 16(1): 69-81.

Bachelier, L. 1900. *Théorie de la speculation*. Reprinted in Cootner (ed.) 1967, The random character of stock market prices, MIT Press, Cambridge, Mass., 17-78.

Ball, R. 1978. *Anomalies in Relationships between Securities' Yields and Yield-Surrogates*. Journal of Financial Economics, 6(2/3): 103-126.

Basu, S. 1975. *The Information Content of Price-Earnings Ratios*. Financial Management, 4(2): 53-64.

Basu, S. 1977. *The Investment Performance of Common Stocks in relation to their Price-Earnings Ratios*. The Journal of Finance, 32(3): 663-182.

Chan, L.C.K., Karceski, J. and Lakonishok, J. 2003. *The Level and Persistence of Growth Rates*. The Journal of Finance, 58(2): 643-184.

Damodaran, A. 2002. *Investment Valuation: Tools and Techniques for Determining the Value of Any Asset*. New York: Wiley.

Dimson, E. and Marsh, P. 1999. *Murphy's Law and Market Anomalies*. Journal of Portfolio Management, 25(2): 53-69.

Dreman, D.N. 2012. *Contrarian Investment Strategies: The Psychological Edge*. New York: Free Press.

Fama, E.F. 1970. *Efficient Capital Markets: A Review of Theory and Empirical Work*. The Journal of Finance, 25(2): 383-417.

Fama, E.F. and French, K.R. 1992. *The Cross-Section of Expected Stock Returns*. The Journal of Finance, 47(2): 427-65.

Fama, E.F. and French, K.R. 1993. *Common Risk Factors in the Returns on Stocks and Bonds*. Journal of Financial Economics, 33(1): 3-56.

Fuller, R.J., Huberts, L.C. and Levinson, M.J. 1993. *Returns to E/P Strategies, Higgeldy Piggeldy Growth, Analysts' Forecast Errors, and Omitted Risk Factors.* Journal of Portfolio Management, 1993(Winter): 13-24.

Graham, B. 1949. *The Intelligent Investor.* New York: Harper Collins.

Graham, B. 1974. *The Future of Common Stocks.* Financial Analysts Journal, 30(5): 20-30.

Graham, B. and Dodd, D. 1934. *Security Analysis.* New York: McGraw-Hill.

Greenblatt, J. 2005. *The Little Book that Beats the Market.* New York: Wiley.

Gregory, A., Harris, R.D.F., and Michou, M. 2001. *An Analysis of Contrarian Investment Strategies in the UK.* Journal of Business Finance and Accounting, 28(9/10): 1193-1228.

Kang, T. 2003. *The Profitability of EP Trading Rule Based on Operating Income.* American Business Review, 21(2): 41-46.

Lakonishok, J., Shleifer, A. and Vishny, R. 1994. *Contrarian Investment, Extrapolation, and Risk.* The Journal of Finance, 49(5): 1541-1578.

Levis, M. 1989. *Stock Market Anomalies.* Journal of Banking and Finance, 13(SI): 675-696.

Little, I.M.D. 1962. *Higgledy Piggledy Growth.* Journal of the Oxford University Institute of Statistics, 24(4): 387-412.

Nicholson, S.F. 1960. *Price-Earnings Ratios.* Financial Analysts Journal, 16(4): 43-45.

Nicholson, S.F. 1968. *Price-Earnings Ratios in Relation to Investment Results.* Financial Analysts Journal, 24(1): 105-109.

Oppenheimer, H.R. 1984. *A Test of Ben Graham's Stock Selection Criteria.* Financial Analysts Journal, 40(5): 68-74.

Piotroski, J.D. 2000. *Value Investing: The Use of Historical Financial Statement Information to Separate Winners from Losers.* Journal of Accounting Research, 38(3): 1-41.

Reinganum, M.R. 1981. *Misspecification of Capital Asset Pricing: Empirical Anomalies Based on Earnings' Yields and Market Values.* Journal of Financial Economics, 9(1): 19-46.

Ross, S.A. 1976. *The Arbitrage Theory of Capital Asset Pricing.* Journal of Economic Theory, 13(3): 341-360.

Sharpe, W.F. 1964. *Capital Asset Prices: A Theory of Market Equilibrium under Conditions of Risk.* The Journal of Finance, 19(3): 425-442.

Shiller, R.J. 1981. *Do Stock Prices Move Too Much to be Justified by Subsequent Changes in Dividends?,* American Economic Review, 71(3), 421-436.

Shiller, R.J. 2001. *Irrational Exuberance. Broadway.*

Slater, J. 1992. *The Zulu Principle: Making Extraordinary Profits from Ordinary Shares.* London: Orion Books.

Slater, J. 1996. *The Zulu Principle: Making Extraordinary Profits from Ordinary Shares.* London: Orion Business.

Strong, N. & Xu, X.G. 1997. *Explaining the Cross-Section of UK Expected Stock Returns.* British Accounting Review, 29(1): 1-23.

# Index

3-factor model (Fama-French), 9, 65–68, 131

## A

adjusted EPS, 15
Aggreko, 87–88
Alternative Investment Market (AIM), 16, 167
amortisation, 13, 14, 15
   definition, 177
analysts forecasts, 16
annual reports, 15, 97
   Haynes Publishing, 29
Arbitrage Pricing Theory (APT), 57–58, 177
assets
   definition, 177–178
   valuation, 39–40
availability heuristic, 48

## B

Bachelier, Louis, 97
balance sheet, 178
Ball, Ray, 59, 60
banking crisis, 21
basic EPS, 15
Basu, Sanjoy, 58–59
behavioural finance, 39, 45, 74
   availability heuristic, 48
Berkshire Hathaway, 43, 44
beta, 56, 67
   and annual returns, 59
   definition, 178
*Beyond the Zulu Principle*, 88

Black–Scholes model, 97
Bolton, Anthony, 46–47
bond issues, 7
bond yield, 25
book value, 178
bubbles, stock market, 9
Buffet, Warren, 15, 40, 147
   criticism of beta, 66–67
   investment methods, 43–44, 47
business cycles, 97

## C

Capital Asset Pricing Model (CAPM), 55–57, 178–179
   arguments against, 59, 61
CAPM. *see* Capital Asset Pricing Model (CAPM)
Child Trust Fund (CTF), 41–42
climate change, 45
Coca-Cola, 39, 40
company accounts, 8, 97
Company REFS, 87
company valuation, 7, 145–146
company year, 107, 110
   definition, 179
   Haynes Publishing, 114
compound interest, 41–42
consolidated accounts, 8
   Haynes Publishing, 29–31
Consolidated Cash Flow statement, 13
Consumption CAPM, 61
contrarian investing, 46
*Contrarian Investment Strategies: The New Psychological Breakthrough*, 43, 46, 58

corporation tax, 9

costs
　calculation, 13–17
　deduction of, 30

cyclically adjusted P/E (CAPE), 97


# D

Damodaran, Aswath, 92

decile portfolios, 100–101
　and the decomposed P/E, 116

decomposed P/E, 77, 107–117
　decomposing the influences on, 109–112
　Fscore and, 161
　Haynes Publishing, 114–115
　testing of, 115–117

depreciation, 13, 14, 15

diluted earnings per share, 15, 30
　definition, 179

Dimson, Elroy, 60, 112

discounted operations, 14

diversification, 81, 135

dividends, 179

dividend yield (DY), 7–8, 25, 180
　value and glamour shares, 39, 40

Dodd, David, 8, 44, 97

dot.com boom, 9

downswing, 39

Dreman, David, 43, 58, 59, 65, 157
　industry-adjusted P/E, 81
　investment methods, 45–46

Dreman Value Management, 45

DuPont analysis, 108

DY. *see* dividend yield (DY)


# E

earnings
　average annual returns (1975-2009), 100
　calculation, 13–17
　data analysis of, 17
　definition, 180
　growth post-Great War, 8
　long-term potential, 97
　manipulation of figures, 17
　operating profit, 13–14
　testing predictability, 91–92, 99–102
　UK positive and growing stocks (1975-2004), 91
　unpredictable rates of growth, 89–91
　volatility, 77

earnings per share
　calculations, 14
　definition, 180–181

earnings yield, 145, 146
　calculation, 25–26
　definition, 181

EBIT, 14–15

EBITDA, 14–15

economic cycles, 97

efficiency (Fscore), 154

Efficient Markets Hypothesis (EMH), 35, 36, 48, 53-55
　value premium and, 58–60, 167–168

equilibrium price, 54, 55

expectation value, 40

expenses, 13

external environment, 77, 107, 109–112


# F

Fama, Eugene, 9, 53, 55, 61, 65, 131

Fidelity Special Situations Fund, 46, 121

Findel, 17

forecast EPS, 16

    calculation, 24

fraud, 17

French, Ken, 9, 65, 131

Fscore (Piotroski), 152–162

    Haynes Publishing, 154–156

    and the P/E, 160–162

    predicting returns, 156–157

    use in the UK, 158–159

FTSE 100 index, 16, 21

    average P/E (1993-2012), 22

FTSE 350 index, 16

Fuller, Russell, 60

funding (Fscore), 153


## G

gilts, 56

glamour shares

    definition, 181

    market performance, 40, 41–42, 47–49

    perception of , 40

    return on investment, 35–36

    value indicators, 39

goodwill, 181

Gotham Capital, 145

Graham, Ben, 8, 43, 97, 135

    investment methods, 44–45, 139–141

Greenblatt, Joel, 82, 131, 135, 145–147

Gross National Product (GNP), 57

gross profit, 13

    definition, 181

Growth at a Reasonable Price (GARP), 82

growth ratio. *see* PEG ratio


## H

Haynes Publishing

    decomposed P/E, 114–115

    EPS (2000-2009), 98

    EPS and P/Es (February 2012), 25

    Fscore (Piotroski), 154–156

    long-term P/E, 98–99

    P/E ratio calculation, 31

    value shares, 40

headline EPS, 15

healthcare sector, 81

*Higgledy Piggledy Growth*, 89

High Minus Low (HML), 65, 66–67

high P/E portfolios, 102–103

historical EPS, 15, 16

    calculation, 30

historical P/E, 24

HSBC, 23

Huberts, Lex, 60


## I

idiosyncratic P/E, 107–108. *see also* naked P/E

Inchcape, 16

    EPS and P/Es (February 2012), 25

income statement, 181–182

    Haynes Publishing, 29

industry-adjusted P/E, 81–82

inflation, 57

Initial Public Offering (IPO), 7–8

intangible assets, 40

    definition, 182

*Intelligent Investor, The*, 43, 44, 66, 139, 147, 170

interest rate risk, 57

Intertemporal CAPM, 61

*Investment Valuation*, 92

*Irrational Exuberance*, 97

## J

Johnston Press, 122


## K

Kang, Tony, 83, 131, 169
Kleeneze, 17


## L

Lakonishok, Josef, 71, 91, 131
Levinson, Michael, 60
linear regression, 113
Little, Ian M.D., 89
*Little Book that Beats the Market, The,*
     135, 145–146
loan covenants, 14
long-run returns, 35
long-term P/E, 77, 97–103, 168
     Haynes Publishing, 98–99
     use of, 99–102
low P/E portfolios, 102–103


## M

'Magic Formula' (Blatt), 131, 145
Margard, James, 82
market capitalisation, 21, 111–112
     Haynes Publishing, 114
     measure of company size, 107
     vs. P/E of companies, 23
market confidence, 21, 23
market prices, 97
market size. *see* market capitalisation
market timing, 110, 112
market-wide P/E, 110, 112
Markowitz, Harry, 56

Marsh, Paul, 60, 112
'Mr. Market', 45


## N

naked P/E, 77, 121–128, 168. *see also*
     idiosyncratic P/E
     Fscore and, 161–162
negative P/Es, 26
net profit. *see* earnings
news, impact on markets, 54–55
Nicholson, Francis S., 47–49, 58


## O

operating income, 16
     P/E and, 82–83, 169
operating profit, 13–14
     calculation, 30
     definition, 182
option pricing model (Black-Scholes), 97
Owens, Ed, 81


## P

payout ratio, 182
PBV. *see* price-to-book value (PBV)
PCF. *see* price-to-cash flow (PCF)
PEG ratio, 87–93
     formula, 87
     predicting earnings growth, 89–91,
          168
     use of, 92–93
pensions, 42
perfect competition, 55
phlogiston theory, 59–60
Piotroski, Joseph, 135–136, 151–163
portfolio theory, 56

industry diversification, 81–82

    stock filters, 139–141

premium shares, 35–36

price, calculation, 21

price movement, 97

price-to-book value (PBV), 9

    in the 3-factor model, 68

    definition, 183

    as method of valuation, 151

    returns by P/E, 48

    value and glamour shares, 39

price-to-cash flow (PCF)

    definition, 183

    value and glamour shares, 39

price-to-sales ratio (PSR)

    definition, 183

    returns by P/E, 48

    value and glamour shares, 39

price-to-tangible book value (PTBV)

    definition, 183

    and the Fscore, 158–159

profit and loss account, 13–17

profit before tax, 14

profit from continuing operations, 14

profitability (Fscore), 152–153

prospective P/E

    calculation, 24

    use in PEG ratio, 88

PSR. *see* price-to-sales ratio (PSR)

PTBV. *see* price-to-tangible book value

    (PTBV)

## R

Rainier Investment Management, 82

random walk, 97

Reinganum, Marc, 60

retained earnings/profit, 184

Return on Assets (ROA), 108

Return on Capital Employed, 145

return on investment, 35–36, 40

    3-factor model (Fama-French), 65

    influencing factors, 107, 109–112

revenue, 184

risk. *see also* volatility

    Arbitrage Pricing Theory, 57

    diversification and, 81

    factors, 57

    Sharpe ratio, 124–125

    SMB and HML factors, 66–67

risk and return, 35–36, 59

    Capital Asset Pricing Model

      (CAPM), 55–57

risk premium, 56, 65

rolling EPS, 15

Ross, Stephen, 57

## S

sales, 13

Scott, Hemmington, 87

sector, company, 107, 110–111, 114, 168

*Security Analysis*, 8, 44, 97, 98

Self Invested personal Pension (SIPP), 42

share prices, 21

Sharpe, Bill, 55–56, 67

Sharpe ratio, 124–125

Shiller, Robert, 39, 97

Shleifer, Andrei, 71, 131

six-monthly interim reports, 15

Slater, Jim, 87, 88

Small Minus Big (SMB), 65, 66

software sector, 111

stock filters, 139–141

stock issues, 7

stock market

    bubbles, 9

    UK, 7

US, 7
stock valuation
dividend yield (DY), 7–8
price-to-book value (PBV), 9
survivorship bias, 48, 58

# T

takeover bids, 54
tangible assets, 39
definition, 184
tax, 9, 14, 15
profit before and after, 30
technology stock boom, 21
time horizons, investor, 55, 56
time-relative P/E, 82

# U

utility companies, 40

# V

value indicators, 39–40, 46, 68
value investment, 35–36, 39–49
value investors, 43–47, 184–185
value premium, 35–36, 41–42, 170
as applied to P/E, 47–49
definition, 185
efficient market theory and, 58–60,
167–168
value shares, 39–40
definition, 185
market performance, 40, 41–42, 47–
49
return on investment, 35–36
value indicators, 39
Vanguard Health Care Group, 81

Vishny, Robert, 71, 131
Vodafone, 23
volatility
definition, 185. *see also* risk
earnings, 77

# W

weighted average shares in issue, 30
definition, 185

# Z

*Zulu Principle*, 87